T0365929

NUJUBUSUWI
SERVING SPIRITUAL STEW

REV. GREGORY WADLEIGH

authorHOUSE®

AuthorHouse™
1663 Liberty Drive
Bloomington, IN 47403
www.authorhouse.com
Phone: 1 (800) 839-8640

Published by AuthorHouse 08/05/2016

ISBN: 978-1-5246-2101-8 (sc)
ISBN: 978-1-5246-2100-1 (e)

Print information available on the last page.

DEDICATION

This book is dedicated to those on the journey back to the place we never really left; which is to say, all of us.

INTRODUCTION

Nujubusuwi. In One Spirit we have a standing joke that we practice Nujubusuwi. That is, we identify as New Jewish Buddhist Sufi Wiccans. We follow the words of Jesus, a Jewish Rabbi who taught a new way to look at the law; we observe the practice of Buddhism in the mindful alleviation of suffering; we are inspired by the unifying principles of Sufism and we are Wiccan in that we actually like the Earth, and not to shock your sensibilities but we think sex is ok too.

Nujubusuwi is the essence of this daily book. Its pages serve up a spiritual stew; meditations which were inspired from all these seemingly disparate spiritual disciplines. We have found that these teachings are actually more related than they may first appear. An underlying principle of unity informs them; the unity of all life, the inter-connectedness of all things, is a the most prominent feature in them all.

The meditations in this book follow an arc. Mixing different views in a seeming random way; they evolve into a totally coherent and unified message which contains and resolves all of the traditions.

JANUARY

Suddenly, I fall from safety
into a place of delicious danger;
passion, rouge on an exotic face,
a thorn lodged in my heart,
the angel of death,
holds a fiery brand...
"burn yourself down" she urges.
Without hesitation I step gladly into the flame.
Burnt up, burnt down by love, I am no longer the
pawn of ego. My darling, your fiery love has washed
my hands of selfishness, cleansed my face of duplicity.
Exquisite Union
has banished my alone-ness.
Words fail to really tell the tale;
Even music cannot play this tune;
Only the whole united heart knows the truth
Of this great love-furnace I have fallen into.

JANUARY 1 – NAMES – I am in awe. We rest in the All-ness of God. How do we give a name to that which is too large and also too small, too much and too little? How do we name the unnamable, and if we make a name how can it suffice? This has been the dilemma for the eons. We have called Divinity be many names, none of which tell the whole story, so we settle for names which most closely fit the occasion. We might call out to God or Allah or Yahweh or Christ. We may address the Dharma, the Tao or the Goddess, Great Spirit, the Redeemer, the Liberator, the Supreme Being, Rama, Ra, or the Ground of All Being. Consider the Hindu tradition "there is only one Rama and he has a thousand names". Others would say God has infinite names. Each of these names resonate in the soul. Feel the stirrings of awe as we consider them, each and every one. As we go through this day let us notice the Divine Presence as we go about our world. Allow whatever names that come to mind be the God Name for this moment.

JANUARY 2 – GOAL – I am focused. Let us surrender to the desires of the heart. We decide how we want our life to be. We examine our aspirations. If we have already written some goals, we set them aside for a moment. If we have not yet written, we take a moment before we commit to a single goal. In that quiet minute, we surrender ego to the creative power within. Let us allow ourselves to be embraced by the universe. We ask the spirit within to guide us in our choices. We allow the heart to shine its light on the path in front of us. After a little while we let our most cherished desires to flow out of us and onto paper. The cliché "You can't have everything" is not a negative statement. It is reflective of material reality. In the world we can have anything, but in truth, not everything. There is not enough time for us to deal with having everything which catches our fancy. Our larger goal, the one which transcends all others, is the return to Oneness, and in achieving this goal we will have everything because we will become everything. In choosing our secondary goals we decide what is important and then put our focus there. The only caution is that none of these secondary goals should be in opposition to the primary goal.

JANUARY 3 – DIVINITY – I am in order. Life is in divine order. With daily surrender to the presence of God within us, we become aware of order in all things. Divine order is just another term for "God's Will", or for Dharma. Cause and effect is in operation. Divine order means that no matter how things appear to be, there is an intention, an opportunity and a pattern of good in the midst of us. When we allow ourselves to feel the underlying unity of all life, it is not hard to see the pattern. Making the right decision is natural. We can be at ease and able to direct our efforts to the greatest effectiveness. We come to understand that we are not just seeing the patterns, we are in the pattern. We are strands in the great tapestry of life, woven together into divine order.

JANUARY 4 – CONNECTED – I am connected to life. Occasionally, we may think we are disconnected or "apart from" never the less, in truth we are linked in the never ending web of life. We have a part to play in creation...our decision is not only whether we will play our role but how much, how effective, how well we will play it. Creation has invested itself in us...there is perfection in us. It doesn't really mean that there is a perfect place for us or a perfect job or a perfect person...it means that the perfection is in us, part of us just as we are part of it. Perfect employment means that we employ the perfection that is in us to a good end...it is of course easier to do when the work we choose compliments your talents and abilities. When we fight against these connections, we become isolated and unhappy in our efforts. So, today we remember we are all a part of...

JANUARY 5 – POSITIVE – I am positive. Today we focus on the positive. "I can't complain, and if I do no one listens anyway". Here is a cliché that is true as long as we don't (complain) but if we do someone is listening... we are and Creation is. Here is where our powerful words can help make more problems. One of the oldest secrets of success is to stop complaining. To complain about people or circumstances shifts our focus from being empowered to being dependent on the actions of others or the perceived vagaries of circumstance. In fact, we really have nothing to complain about. We have made our lives and we go on making them with each decision. So let's take responsibility, stop complaining and focus on the positive.

JANUARY 6 – ACCEPTANCE – I am responsible. Today we accept responsibility for life. Excuses are just another way to complain. We know that the "dog ate my homework" excuse was always preposterous, sounding implausible the first time someone used it, but what about all of the other excuses that get used daily? "I was so busy...", "I just am not feeling that well...", "I guess I just don't have 'it' today". Let's not make any excuses. If in the course of the day we make a mistake, we take responsibility for it in as straightforward a manner as possible. If someone else makes a mistake, it is probably better to say nothing at all. Even if we had nothing to do with the shortcoming, it cannot help to point to others. We accept what is, and then do our best to facilitate a solution. No excuses.

JANUARY 7 – MOVE – I am moving forward. We keep moving forward and upward. When things seem hard we remind ourselves to keep moving forward, to remember that the path of life is ever upward. Sometimes it seems like it would be so easy to just give up…to stop trying. Let's not be confused, there is a difference between giving up the ego and giving up the ghost. When an endeavor is only about money, property or prestige, surrender is in order. When the contest is against our own best efforts then the only regret is in the quitting. No quitting. If the work becomes difficult, we try to relax into it. Struggle may seem necessary but it is not when we remember the words "Easy does it, but do it".

JANUARY 8 – AWARE – I am aware. We can sense the power of creation as it moves through us. As we sit quietly allowing our awareness of the presence of God to grow stronger we feel the power that is within us, between us and all around us. Today, let's make a decision to carry this feeling with us when we get up and out into the world. A relaxed sense of power, a focused ability to create which continually flows through us. Nothing to worry about we are immersed in the river of life and the water is warm. Creation comes easily to us when we relax into it, because we are children of God and we know that the "apple doesn't fall far from the tree".

JANUARY 9 – REALITY – I am doing my part. When Jesus first began to preach the good news of the kingdom of God, he was asked: What is the kingdom like? He said "It is like a man who sows a seed on the earth: he goes about his business, and day by day the seed sprouts and grows, he doesn't know how. The earth bears fruit by itself, first the stalk, then the ear, then the full grain in the ear. And when the grain is ripe, the man goes in with his sickle, because it is harvest time." Over this past week we may have fallen short in our pursuit of our goals and resolution. Remember that our number one role and the number one goal is to be conscious co-creator with God. So, as Jesus says further on: "Seek first the kingdom of heaven and then all of these will be added unto you."

JANUARY 10 – GIVE – I am giving. I give myself freely to life. It is a new day and a new life. I am open to new possibilities. I give myself freely, but I give with prudence. I take a moment and ask for guidance, so that I might be sure that what I give is for the common good. As I learn to be open and fearless in my giving, even more opportunities present themselves. This is a new year as well as a new day. Really no different than any other day except I can use it as a demarcation point. It is a symbol of new beginnings and so I embrace it. I consider the things I wish to eliminate and the things I wish to enhance. I focus on allowing the Good in me to come forth in fresh new ways. This is a new day and I will make myself new in it.

JANUARY 11 – FIDELITY – I am true. Today we focus on fidelity. We are attempting to be faithful to the values and principles which we hold dear. There may be many things calling for our attention but we stay focused on our main goal. We will, therefore be guided in that which we are to do. As we move through the day there will be times that we are tempted to take the "easy way" out of a situation. We know that there are no spiritual shortcuts, so we stay on track. We practice the principles that we know will bring about the best solution. We give love and kindness wherever and whenever we find the opportunity. Aware of the omnipresence of Spirit and the power of principle we flow through the day. In this way we find inner peace and become a force for Good in the world.

JANUARY 12 – SPONTANEOUS – I am spontaneous. Be aware of the eternal moment. We now understand how precious each of these moments is, so we keep the mind centered. We release any angry, regretful thoughts of the past and we let go of all fear of the future. We are free to live in the present. As we go through the day living each moment fully, as it occurs the joy of God fills the heart. Spontaneous life springs forth from this joy. We are filled with a great energy to carry out our present mission. We are fully involved with living. Focused on what's going on right now we can clearly see what needs to be done right now. We become inspired and by acting on that inspiration we become a shining examples for others. Let our affirmation be: I stay in this day, I live in this moment, I focus on right now.

JANUARY 13 – BUSINESS – I am involved in God's business. Jewish tradition says that the children of the father can't become son (daughter) of the father until they enter into the father's business. We are all children of God; to become conscious sons or daughters of God we enter into God's business. Our Father is in the love business, lovingly creating the universe every moment. So God is minding God's business all the time; creating life, creating love. Doing likewise we become sons of Spirit – we enter God's business and then we mind it. Today, we see ourselves as part of the creation business. In all that we do let's be creative. Take a fresh look at everything. Bring love to life and life to love. After all, it's our inheritance.

JANUARY 14 – ABLE – I am able to bring my talents and abilities to bear. We can accomplish great things when we apply our temporarily special gifts. It is our responsibility to decide when and how to express our creativity. We get to choose to bring our creative talents into everything that we do. Accessing the indwelling spirit of God and focusing our thoughts on serving others we are able to share our gifts in the most effective ways. We generate a loving aura around us and that creates a harmonious atmosphere. We each have a unique combination of talents that is unlike anyone else's. There is no need to compare our abilities to those of others, we just focus on how we can be most helpful right now.

JANUARY 15 – CONCENTRATE – I am concentrating. Let's concentrate on the task at hand. We give it our undivided attention. As we focus on doing what is in front of us, we take satisfaction in doing our best. We can accomplish whatever we set out to do in a creative, elegant way. Whether the task of the day seem minor or major, underwhelming or overwhelming we keep our attention centered on the larger issue of service in all things. We simply renew our commitment to Goodwill and we follow the guidance of Spirit. Temptations concerning the controversy of the day are set aside as we remember what we are really about. Worries and concerns fall away as we put our energy into accomplishing the work of this moment. We concentrate on what is in front of us and much success is assured.

JANUARY 16 – GOOD – I am for good. We stand for Good rather than against something "bad". Jesus said "Resist not evil". That will be our focus of the day. This does not mean that we ignore injustice, pain and suffering in the world. We do not deny the effectiveness of social activism. We just recognize that when we begin to fight against some seeming evil that we are actually draining our own power and adding power to the thing that we are against. We can, instead, attend to the positive goal. If we find upset in some injustice instead of fighting against it, we determine what the opposite of the situation is, and we work with the power of Good in us to bring that about. We visualize the issue, behavior, or need healed and then we go into action to make it so. It may seem subtle difference but it makes a great difference in the outcome. When we work for the good we are building momentum for the desired end. Today, the vision we hold generates the energy required to bring that vision into manifestation.

JANUARY 17 – ART – I am an artist. Today we put energy into the things that are important. Creation is an energy intensive business. We will need to be selective as to what we invest power in. During the day there are many things which vie for our attention, let us choose wisely. Working to fulfill a precious purpose we do not want to become side-tracked. This day is like a block of marble waiting for the artist to release its glory. We will be artists, deliberately sculpting an idea or a dream into a masterpiece. We can make our life a work of art. There is little time to dally with distractions. This is not to say that we can't take time for recreation, because recreation is part of a joyful life, we just try to make sound decisions about what we will do with our time. This attention to detail will pay great dividends, our mission will be fulfilled and life will be artful.

JANUARY 18 – TRUST – I am trusting God's loving spirit. We have heard it said: Seek first to understand, then to be understood. In the past we may have missed the true meaning in another's words simply because we were not really listening. If we do not understand it is very difficult to be understood. In relationships at home, work or in the community the success of our service is determined by how well we communicate. We can be better communicators when we trust God's loving spirit to direct us. Listening to others, we learn to listen with love. We rely on our inner guide, not appearances, to reveal the true meaning of someone's words or actions. Trusting in Spirit, we need not fear misunderstanding. We are inspired to do and say the right things at just the right time.

JANUARY 19 – OPEN – I am open. Open minded and open hearted we understand. We radiate an aura of love, which projects friendliness and objectivity to all those around us. We are sensitive to the needs of others, and know when to bring things out into the open. As we listen carefully to what people have to say we open up to their ideas. God speaks to and through everyone, we just have to be willing to hear. This willingness opens the way for understanding, which lays the groundwork for empathy. Empathy allows us to relate in a loving, non-threatening way. We can share openly and as we do, we become more relaxed and are able to listen deeply so that we gain a new perspective. Open and receptive to the divine guidance that comes to us from others, we find that they also become open and receptive to what we have to say.

JANUARY 20 – REAL – I am real. Today, let us be genuine. We may have felt it was safer to show the world a false face; perhaps we thought we would be better accepted by playing a role not our own. We will do much better in all regards if we remain authentic. Anytime we feel "less than or more than" others we have slipped away from reality. These delusions will interfere with our ability to be ourselves and thus find real success. Deceptive mental survival skills are not needed on the spiritual path. We are the good of Creation expressing as us, so we should just allow that good to express through us. Let us go forth and be who we really are.

JANUARY 21 – FEARLESS – I am fearless. Apparently there is much to fear in the world, evidence abounds. Evolution has provided us with a biological imperative that is sympathetic to alarm. In the material world there is much danger, we have designed it that way. In Spirit there is no danger, we are cared for and protected from all harm. The body is vulnerable and spirit is not. Ultimately the body will fail, spirit will not. To the extent that we identify with the body we will be afraid; and it is pretty sure that we will from time to time identify with the body. Even so, we are following a path that leads from fear to courage to fearlessness. When fear shows itself, we courageously act in spite of it. In this way the fear fades and eventually comes no more. Inspired by those who live fearlessly we emulate them in our approach to life. We will in turn become examples to those who are caught up in fear. Remember the adage: "There are only two things in life: love and fear, and fear is just a lie I tell myself." So as we identify more with spirit we will live more in Love where there is no fear.

JANUARY 22 – EQUALITY – I am equal. Temporarily we are unique, just like everyone else. The power of Creation is expressing through us as us. We are experiencing an individualization of the divine, and so is everyone else. Do not allow thoughts of superiority or inferiority to cloud the mind. Welcome diversity and understand that God is making God-self known in and through us all. Equal we are and equal we will be. There is no need to strive to be better than someone else. In the material world we need only compete with our own best efforts, in Spirit we don't compete at all. In all that we do, we surrender authority to God and then proceed with whatever service we are guided to. We then take responsibility for our work and our life; we take responsibility for that which we make.

JANUARY 23 – TRUE – I am true. It is time for us to live in a manner that reflects that which we believe. We will consider what is truly important to us and put our attention on that. We will reflect on the values that we hold dear and we will then act in that manner. Approaching our brothers and sisters with kindness and compassion we will show respect and give love. We will speak the positive, uplifting words which will build relationships and bind us all together in an endeavor of goodwill. People sense that we are at peace and they are drawn to us. As we focus on being ourselves, we are able to let love flow easily from us and we find that even more flows back to us.

JANUARY 24 – FOUNDATIONAL – I am a part of. We are at the foundation of creation. The spirit that we are a part of is the entirety of God. Contrary to our fears and delusion we cannot be separate from our source. While we may not yet believe it, we can visualize that Creation is built on us, and we are built of Creation. We can at least imagine that we stand at the beginning and at the end. Wherever we seem to go, God goes with us. We actually never really go anywhere because we are already everywhere! The body seems to travel, and since that is the experience we are presently having we may as well cooperate. We can however remember that the body is neutral and it will reflect that which is in our mind. So, in our "travels" we can allow the body to reflect Good or project ill it is really up to us. Accepting that we share the foundation of the universe with all life we will find it easier to act accordingly.

JANUARY 25 – ALL – I am in all. God…God is…God is all there is…God is all there is and nothing else is. As we become quiet and centered in prayer, we become deeply aware of the presence of God within us. This awareness of God within us is just the beginning. Sitting in silence or moving through the world we establish a vision, we begin to notice the divine presence in others, looking more intently we see that this presence is everywhere, in everyone and in everything. With continued practice we can see God in situations and circumstances. We no longer need to feel that we are at the mercy of circumstance or events. We will notice the holy aura about and around people regardless of how they act. The world of our experience is becoming more and more beautiful. We are the spirit which fills us. We see the magnificence of God in all outer symbols. We look with new eyes; we hear with new ears. Connected to life in uncountable ways, we rejoice in the oneness of all things. We now know that God is all there is.

JANUARY 26 – SONG – I am singing. Rumi says: "All religions, all this singing, is one song. The differences are just illusion and vanity. The sun's light looks a little different on this wall than it does on that wall...but it's still one light." Today, let us sing a new song, a song of one-ness. We can release old ways knowing that the light coming from the sun is but a symbol for the light of God that is shining out from the eyes of those around us and from all living things. We need not threatened by the beliefs of others. We really can disagree without being disagreeable. We understand that in faith no one is wrong and we don't have to make ourselves right. All of the hurt done in the name of religion will eventually be seen as futile and misguided. Errors in practice will work themselves out. All paths lead to God; all these religions are indeed streams flowing into the ocean of Creation...

JANUARY 27 – GOOD – I am good. In the past we may have thought of ourselves as being less than good. The truth is that as children of God, who is all Good, we cannot but be good. So let's stop arguing with ourselves about it. We are Spirit and that is good, we are Mind and that is good, we are not really bodies, but the bodies we seem to have can certainly reflect the good that is us. So we can safely say that body, mind and spirit are all good. The power of Creation is that which makes up our spirit, it is the fire that sparks the mind and it is the energy that enlivens the body. Allowing the body to emulate the good of spirit is the most certain way to keep it healthy and too see that its functions are holy. So we sanctify the body, we do not deny it or denigrate it, we do not starve or neglect it and we do not abuse or mistreat it. Our mind is part of divine Mind and as such it is alert and responsive, and because of its sacred connection it is always receiving holy thoughts. Let us choose to focus on these holy thoughts, releasing any negativity. Remembering that we are all good, our spirit soars, it is caught up in the joy of creation, and it flies with angels.

JANUARY 28 – PRAYER -- I am praying for others. Our prayer for others binds us all together. We remember that love, in its pure form, is our ability to connect with others and our desire that only good come to them. Affirming that love, we extend kindness in our thoughts towards people. We consider those who are close and those who seem far away. We affirm that they will experience the presence of God in all that they do. We pray that they be happy, peaceful, and free from suffering. We see this Presence caring for them, going with them where we cannot go. The love of Creation heals them and makes them whole. We know that they can overcome any challenge through the light of Spirit in them. We see healed, whole, and free.

JANUARY 29 – MOMENT – I am in the moment. This moment is the one. This one moment in time is the only real moment. This is the holy moment. This is the time when creation happens. God is always here, right now, involved totally with the business of love. God is building up and binding together in this moment. Right now this power and presence of God is available to us. Yesterday's presence has past, tomorrow's presence is yet to be. Focus on living right now, centered in this holy moment. We are continually strengthened as we focus on the power of God that is now. Releasing all past regrets and resentments, we are at peace. Letting go of all fear of the future, we are at peace. We are at peace right now.

JANUARY 30 – FRUITFUL – I am fruitful. In past times the instruction "Be fruitful and multiply" seemed to be an order from God to populate the planet. This idea has done more to destroy the quality of life for many people than any other single concept. Families and nations are held in poverty and lack by their inability to care for their members. The environment is put at risk and many times damaged by this run-away train of overpopulation. This is certainly not what God intended. In truth when it was written, it was very important to the Hebrew people that they procreate. They were in exile and had hopes of restoring themselves and their culture to its former state. The thought of course being, if there are more of us we can overcome our enemies and our circumstances. Today, however, we know that the principle of fruitfulness means much more than reproducing as many humans as possible. Fruitfulness is the direct application of our creativity. Let's concentrate on allowing the good that is in our hearts and minds to come forth in new and wonderful ways. Today, let us be truly fruitful and multiply our blessings.

JANUARY 31 – STEWARDSHIP – I am a good steward. Our dominion is a sacred stewardship. When the text of Genesis advises that man has dominion over the earth and the creatures therein, it really is not suggesting that we have the right to decimate the planet. This "masters of the world" mindset was the prominent view in past times, it was incorrect then and it is even more misguided today. We know this seems apparent, but many of our brothers still believe that this dominion means conquering the earth and subjugating the other living things. We have made great strides in many areas of science and technology and many of these advances have come at the expense of Mother Earth. Today, we have the technical ability to begin to reverse this trend. We have the mental acuity to see the folly of past ways and we have the spiritual awareness that will lead us to stewardship. Let us affirm our oneness with all Creation, which is to say with God. Let us understand that we are responsible for the health and welfare of home and the other living things that share it with us.

FEBRUARY

Bittersweet

Take from me
This taste
Remove this
Suffering.
Oh, I love
The warm
Sweetness
As it occurs;
Then mistakenly
Try to grasp
And hold it.
Bitter it turns
Then cold.

FEBRUARY 1 – LIFE – I am filled with life. God is not some great man sitting off somewhere beyond the sky, observing the comings and goings of his subjects. Consider rather that God is the very spirit of life. God is the overarching principle and power of creation. The whole of all life is the essence of God. To believe otherwise is to be caught in a web of manipulation by organizations which are designed to keep power over people. When we think of the supreme being as a ruler who judges us…as a divine benefactor who sometimes dispenses good things or, alternately as a punisher who demands and takes retribution, we cheat ourselves and we put our world at risk. Our Father/Mother is the foundation of all things. All things spring forth from this Divinity. All life is sacred and should be revered. Today, let us understand that the creation acts through us and as us, not to us. God is not going to rescue us from the folly we have perpetrated upon the world, but God expressing through us can restore the planet and our oneness with it. We are filled with the life of God, let us express it through love.

FEBRUARY 2 – BREATH – I am the breath of God. God breathes in us. Consider the words of Ezekiel 36 v1-15. See how it is a meditation on death leading to life. In this moment allow the Holy Spirit to come over your consciousness. Visualize a dry valley, seemingly dead. The valley is full of bones, these are the bones of our lost hopes and dreams. The Spirit questions: "Can these bones ever live?" We answer: "You know, spirit." Spirit says "Tell these bones that the breath of God is entering them and causing them to live. Sinews and flesh and skin are covering them and breath is coming into them." The breath of God comes from the four corners and causes these aspirations to come back to life. All of our starved and abandoned ideas and ideals are now vital and alive. As with Ezekiel and the whole house of Israel, all of us (those who strive with God) rise up knowing that though we felt cut off from God and life, we are One and we live again.

FEBRUARY 3 – SPIRIT – I am inspired (in spirit). Spirit moves over the face of the deep. In Genesis (1:2) we find the reference to God as spirit hovering over the face of the deep. Bishop Spong suggests that this refers to God as "mother hen brooding over her nest to bring forth life". God, not as some external force but rather a power which is found in and emerges from all life. Viewing the material world in a symbolic way we can think of evolution as the activity of God, continuing to bring forth new life. We know that life, new and old, is One. The unity of all life is the law of life. There is no way for us to separate ourselves from any other life. We share the same DNA and same motive power. The spirit that generates our energy does the same for all life. Spirit moves over the face of the deep...this spirit moves in and through us all.

FEBRUARY 4 – NATURE – I am one with nature. Gone are the days when we can consider ourselves apart from nature. Our supposed punishment for eating of the fruit of the tree of knowledge of good and evil was banishment from the harmony of the Garden of Eden. The scripture tells us that we must suffer adversity and adversarial relations with the Earth. What really happened? The "fruit" was an idea that we digested; a thought that we were separate from each other and from God. It intimated that there was something other than God. That we had our existence apart from Him. This event was original sin, the first mistake, the error that led us to an illusory uniqueness, and it was all a lie. God was One and God is One. We were one with God and we are one with God. Let us return to this knowing…one with God really does mean being one with nature.

FEBRUARY 5 – GOD – I am. God is…I am. God is the source from which all life flows. We remember to respect all of life knowing that it comes directly from God. Since God is the source of love, we are love. We can feel our connection to all living things and our desire that only good to come to all living things. God is Whole…we are holy. We are called to revere all of Creation, so we care for the earth with all of its living things. Conservation is an endeavor to preserve. We take care, paying attention to how we use and what we spend. To waste as little as possible and to save as much as possible, that is our responsibility. To be in alignment with goodwill we become steward of all that is given into our care. Worship means being in awe of creation, destruction can never be reconciled with worship.

FEBRUARY 7 – QUIET – I am quiet. Today, let's quiet the all of the inner noise and focus on the ongoing wonder of creation. God is still speaking. God is still speaking the universe. God is speaking the Word. From John chapter one verses 3-5 we read: "The Word was with God in the beginning, through it all things came to be, not one thing had its being but through it. All that came to be had life in it…" And so it continues today, all beings and all things are the words of God, and as Meister Ekhert says "Books about God". All creatures are gladly doing the best they can to express God. God is constantly speaking only one thing… In this one utterance he speaks his Son and at the same time the Holy Spirit and all creatures…There where God speaks the creatures, there God is. So, today let's pay attention and listen to creation being spoken in existence…today let's be quiet and observe.

FEBRUARY 8 – LIFE – I am totally involved with life. God lives in all. Let us observe the totality of creation in all things. As Thich Nhat Hanh reminds us: "When we look into the heart of a flower, we see clouds, sunshine, minerals, time, the earth, and everything else in the cosmos it it. Without clouds, there could be no rain, and there would be no flower. Without time, the flower could not bloom. In fact, the flower is made entirely of non-flower elements; it has no independent, individual existence." So it is with us we are made entirely of non-people elements and we have no independent, individual existence. We live and move and have our being inside the totality of creation. Let us relax into that sense of oneness. Today, we observe the totality of creation in everything. We see God in all; expressing as all.

FEBRUARY 9 – AWAKEN – I am waking up. Wake Up! A Buddha is someone who is awake. Today we can wake to the present moment and the present place. Awake and aware of creation in every moment, we see existence for the miracle that it is and we pay attention to the unfoldment of it. We are awake, aware and focused in the now. Thich Naht Hanh: "The miracle is not to walk on water or in the air. The miracle is to walk on the green earth in the present moment". Our practice then is to be in the present moment, to be aware that we are here and now. We realize that the only moment to be alive in is the present moment. And of course Jesus was saying the same thing when he told us: "The kingdom of God is closer than hands and feet, closer than your breath...". So today, we wake up to see things differently, to realize how close to heaven we are.

FEBRUARY 10 – INSIGHT – I am insightful. Ignorance is sometimes described as absence of light. Really the light cannot be absent, ignorance is just a shadow. Ignorance is simply not knowing. It is lack of awareness. When we bring a light into a dark room, the darkness is dispelled. There is light enough in us to brighten any dark place. As we allow the light in us to recognize the light in others, we move from ignorance to insight. We actually bring the "not knowing" into the light of knowledge. When we see the through the darkness in situations, I move from ignorance to insight. Shakymuni said "Be you lamps unto yourselves". Enlightenment is evidenced by how we shine. When we see as Thich Naht Han points out: "The trees, the birds, the violet bamboo, and the yellow chrysanthemums are all preaching the Dharma that Shakymuni preached 2500 years ago. We can be in touch with him through any of these. He is the living Buddha, always available. The road to Buddhahood is open to all." Today let's look past appearance to the essence of things, to the Buddha in all.

FEBRUARY 11 – LIFE – I am in the light. Light lives in us and as us. The Christ (Buddha) in us is the essence of all life. That life is the light of people, a light that shines in the dark, a light that no darkness can overpower. From the Gospel of John: "You are the light of the world" as we follow the light, we do not walk in the dark for we actually are the light of life. When we go out into the world, we bring the light with us. The Word (creation of God) is the true light that enlightens all men; and He (the Christ) is coming into the world. From Thomas we hear: Jesus said: If they say to you "Where are you from?" say to them: "We came from the light there, where the light was, by itself. It stood boldly and manifested itself in our image." The light that shines in us is the light that is over all things. When we surrender to the light, we are that light.

FEBRUARY 12 – BRIGHT – I am bright. Our thoughts are bright prayers. We should remember that all of our thoughts are prayers and they project our desires and intentions. The heart emits waves of love. Let us focus today on combining the light from our thoughts with the love from the heart. The purple light of Power, the blue light of Faith, the silvery thread of Will, a wisp of yellow in light of Wisdom, gold Understanding, olive green Order twists and turns together with russet of Elimination, spinning together with spring green Strength, flowing into the pink light of Love and the bright red ribbon of Life, sky blue cord of Vision coming together with Orange zeal. We are merging all these individual light-strands into the beginnings of a new fabric of creation. Thread by thread, moment by moment we weave a new situation, a new opportunity, a new life, becoming the white light of Christ. This is your light, your life, your bright thoughts being the Son of God.

FEBRUARY 13 – RELEASE – I am releasing problems. Today we give our problems to the light. All of our worries and personal concerns we give to the light. Take a moment right now and allow some ongoing problem to come to mind. What is the biggest unresolved issue in your life? Oh yeah, there it is…yes, yes, just look at it there…all ugly and…dark…and…big. Know that it cannot harm the real you. Now, just start to shine the Christ light on this big wart of problem. That light in you is yours to direct. Bring your problem to the light. When the issue is totally involved in the light, address it, ask it what gift is has for you. What is its purpose, what is its job? Allow the problem to speak directly to you. Take a moment to consider what has been said. Now, give thanks for the issue, for the problem, thank it for its gift to you. Your light, your enlightenment is now healing and resolving this issue, let go and allow it to do its work.

FEBRUARY 14 – EMBRACE – I am holding others in the light. Let us embrace others with the light that shines in us. We give our loved ones to the light. Is there someone we are worried about? Is there someone who is in need of help? Someone in need of healing? Oh, there they are…you see them now. Sometimes we think that we have to save other people. We feel we are responsible for saving them from pain. Embracing others with light is not about rescuing them. We cannot cheat people out of their pain or their joy. What we can do though, is send the light of love in us out from us to touch and merge with the light in them. See it happening right now. That Christ light, that enlightened Buddha nature is reaching out from you to embrace your loved one. Notice how your light comes together with their light and how the two together become brighter. This is a blessing for you and a blessing for them. From now on, whenever you are concerned about someone else just send light. Send the healing light from your heart to theirs…and then observe what happens.

FEBRUARY 15 – ENLIGHTEN – I am enlightened? The news of the day…the disaster of the week…played and replayed on television, on the radio. Woeful tales of degradation and disaster. Sometimes it is hard to take… well today we stop taking in hurt and start giving out light. We start giving love for fear. Make a commitment to give the light of love to every need you see or hear of today. Establish a habit of watching and listening to the news with the eyes and ears of the enlightened being that you are. Instead of reacting with fear and loathing, give love and understanding. See wounds being healed, families made whole, people restored to the sanity of oneness. Allow the light that is in you to go forth touching all of those in need, those you know and those you don't know. Again notice how your light seems to ignite the light of others. See the whole world surrounded in the light of God. That light is our shared light.

FEBRUARY 16 – HOST – I am a good host. Sometimes it is comforting to think about God as being more personal than abstract; just remember that this is symbolic of the reality that lies beyond the prose. I know that the altar is in my mind but my body seems to have become the house of God. Yes, God took up residence in my body. I can't remember when, but I feel Her there now. It is a joyous knowing. Maybe He just moved in recently or probably She has always lived in me and I didn't realize it. In any case I know it now and it makes me happy. I have decided to be a good host, so I am fixing up the place. I am being careful to take in the proper amount of quality fuel; exercising and getting enough rest. I also continue to feed my mind by reading and sometimes I give the old boy a treat by taking us out to a movie. I am having some really good conversations with Her and now She seems be talking back quite a bit more. I am so happy to have the company…and I don't have so much fear anymore that He might move out. I actually think She's here for keeps, but that doesn't mean I'm going to take anything for granted…so I am going to continue to be a good host.

FEBRUARY 17 – BUILD – I am a builder. Today, we focus on building up. The great light in us is a blessing. This energy in us is a force and a power that works to add greatness to our families and our communities. We bless everyone we meet with this energy. We do not concern ourselves with petty jealousy. Although the advertisers may tell us that we need to get the things that some others have, we ignore their calls. We cease comparing ourselves with others. We no longer feel superior or inferior to anyone. We release all envy. We celebrate good fortune, our own and everyone else's. We are the builders of community and our attention is now focused on building up not tearing down. We accept praise with a simple thank you; and we give praise for the goodness we observe. We recognize the light in everyone and we bless them for it. We are builders and we are building a new and better life for us all.

FEBRUARY 18 – ONE – I am one. We are all one with the One. God is in all and all is in God. Is this pantheism or is it real monotheism? It is the observation that God is the whole of everything. All things exist in and from God. Today let us observe God. See God in everything, everywhere, and everyone. We cannot be lost nor can God be lost to us. As we practice this idea all through the day, we remain conscious of our oneness with God and when we think self, we shift our thoughts to the larger Self. When we think of others we think of them being a part that same larger Self. Whatever name is spoken we will hear God. In this way we can transcend the mundane, giving divine service to the whole of Creation and ultimately realizing that we are truly united with It in all that we do. Happiness arises when we remember that we are one with the One. We are at peace and we bring peace. Love comes to us and love goes forth from us.

FEBRUARY 19 – WISDOM – I am thinking through my heart. Wisdom shines through us as we combine judgment with love. Release intellect into the keeping of the heart. Today we will direct all of our thoughts through the heart. The wisdom of God comes only when we bring our power of Judgment together with the power of Love. Love lives in the heart, it is the power that binds together, the power that wants only good for all of creation, when we filter all our thoughts through this aura of love we become wise. We can then use wisdom to serve life. Mind and heart become one in pursuit of God's will. The masculine and the feminine come into balance and then that balance can be extended into the world. Wisdom attracts those in need of it. Wise, we become an influence to those around us. Today, let us be the Sophia of God living and working for the good of all.

FEBRUARY 20 – HEART – I am in my heart. Today, I place a hand or sometimes both hands over my heart when I pray. This helps connect the energy centers in the hands with the heart center. Throughout the day I allow the love in my heart to flow through my hands in all my endeavors. By letting the great power of my heart to express itself through my actions, I become an asset to the world. My contributions are strong and right, because they come from the mind but travel through the heart and in that way all of the self-seeking ego motives are filtered out. Ibn alArbi teaches: "In the heart my small part becomes the universe. You thought yourself a part, small; whereas in you there is a universe, the greatest. That is to say, you think of yourself as a small thing, whereas in you there is hidden the biggest of the universes…" Today, I place my hands over my heart when I pray, and the love of God flows out through me to the world.

FEBRUARY 21 – BEING – I am. God is wonder, I am wonderful. God is love, I am loving. This is the truth of my being. Sometimes it is easy to get off track. We may lose sight of our intimate connection with God. We may begin to think that we are less than others. We may think of ourselves as somehow inferior. In the fear that this might be true, our tendency may be to act as if we are more than, or superior to. Our ego may even tell us that we are defective but on the other hand that it (the ego) is super-effective. Let us return to sanity and remember that we are part of god, part of goodness itself and as such we are enough and good enough. Take a moment now and on the next in-breath silently say "God is…" and on the out-breath say aloud "I am". God is strength…I am strong. This is quite powerful and will pass both time and trouble. God is, I am.

FEBRUARY 22 – CREATE – I am creative. Today, I will be creative. My nature is to be inventive. My nature is to allow imagination to unfold into new ideas and then to see them becoming new things and then to put this vision into practice by taking action. I see myself inspired and then putting hands and feet to my inspiration. Today, I will listen to my intellect and then I will allow the idea to enter the intuitive side of my brain. I may sing my idea; I may draw or paint it…. I may make it into a dance…or perhaps allow it to flow from me as poetry. In this way I allow the full creative power that is in me to be expressed.

FEBRUARY 23 – PROPHET – I am the prophet of my own life. My intuition is strong and growing stronger. I sometimes have a sense that cannot be fully explained in words. It is an inner knowing. It is an ability to feel, what should happen next. I am becoming more and more able to take a chance on this sense. I am able to use my intellect but then I am able to breathe the life of spirit back into the ideas. I let go of fear and move into life with an excitement and expectation. I understand that sometimes there is danger in acting on intuition, if I feel that what I am about to do is an expression of goodwill, I know it is worth the risk. I am the prophet of my own life.

FEBRUARY 24 – JUSTICE – I am just. I support divine justice. Divine justice is cause and effect in action. I understand that when I set events in motion there will be costs and consequences. The results could be called karma or they could be called rewards and punishments. I know that if I begin with concern for the common welfare and a sense of responsibility for those around me, my actions will generally bring good to all. If I do not have this focus, the consequences will become apparent. I will be on the outside looking in and I will cause harm to myself and others. Because divine justice is always present, the opportunity for good will be present even in the midst of a calamity. Each of us has the ability to choose the good no matter what our behavior or someone else's behavior has been.

FEBRUARY 25 – ANGELS – I am aware of angels. There are angels among us. We may see them or feel them in many different ways. Some angels may be people, or memories, or even the essence of those who have passed. They are loving powers which seek to help; they are divine ideas seeking to express through us. There is great symbolism in Sheldrake's suggestion that the sun is one great angel and so are the other heavenly bodies. Angels are divine power coming to us in some form which is designed to guide and assist us in some way. If we turn our attention to them, we will become aware that there is a constant stream of angels passing in front of us.

FEBRUARY 26 – RELEASE – I am letting go. I release all superstition. I am not superstitious. I understand the difference between spiritual things and the belief in magic. I know that seeming evil is just the misapplication of creative power, not the tool of some malevolent force. The "Devil" does not really exist as some super evil person or even a fallen angel. Satan is just one of the voices of the ego. I know that I am capable of "evil" but that I am not trapped into it. Cause and effect, the law of dharma is always in effect. I can decide to work for good and release all superstition.

FEBRUARY 27 – MELD – I am melding. My being is integrated and balanced. My mind and body are one. The twin hemispheres of my brain are now united. My intellect and my intuition are wed, and this marriage is an antidote to vanity. Vanity has been telling me that I am less than some and more than others...it is a lie...all are of equal value to the universe. I am of two minds no longer, my being is healed and whole. My male and female natures have come together and are working in harmony to create and justice and equality...right judgment and compassion. The Father and the Mother have become one in me and in that union a new world is born.

FEBRUARY 28 – EQUALITY – I am practicing equality. We are all equal. Genesis 1:27 states. "So God created humankind in his image, in the image of God he created them; male and female he created them." There is a totally different account (the rib story) in Genesis 2:22. We know that when there is conflict we rely on the principle of love. So, which story speaks more to your heart? Equality just feels right, doesn't it? We remember that "God is spirit" and that is the image in which we were created. The spirit of the Ever-living dwells in us, whatever our body type. All, each and every one of us is of equal value to Spirit. Actually all of us are just that, Spirit incarnate. Today, let us practice this equality in our hearts and our actions.

FEBRUARY 29 – CORRECTION – I am correcting course. In the spirit of the purpose of this day which only occurs every four years as a mathematical correction, we make our own corrections. Today we take a moment to examine our activities of the past two months. Have we lost sight of our goals or fallen short of our practice, take this moment to refocus and recommit. Whatever errors we may have made we now look for solutions. We can amend our thoughts and our behaviors to align them with our heartfelt goals. We will do well to remember that part of effective practice is to make adjustments to various routines that might not be working.

MARCH

Deny not
The body,
In some
Vain attempt
At sainthood.
Rather be
With it in
Experience.
If it reports
Pleasure
Take that
As it seems;
Likewise
What pain
Presents.

Listen only
To this:
Neither pursue
Nor avoid
It's requests.
Be in the flow
Of the material.
Receive it as
It comes, trying
All the while
To observe

Unattached.
Notice if ego's
Promises are kept.

Only then
After some
Time can
The body
And the world
Be freed.
Release coming
When the
Dreamer awakes
And realizing
The dream,
Says "I, you,
He, she, we...
Don't want
This anymore"

MARCH 1 – WISDOM – I am wise. We are immersed in the wisdom of God. This wisdom has been named Sophia in the Jewish tradition. Wisdom shines through us as we combine judgment with love. Let us release intellect into the keeping of our hearts. Today we direct all thoughts through the heart. The wisdom of God comes only when we bring our power of Judgment together with the power of Love. Love lives in our heart, it is the power that binds together, the power that wants only good for all of creation, when we filter all thoughts through this aura of love, we become wise. We use our wisdom to serve life. Mind and heart become one in pursuit of God's will. The masculine and the feminine are then balanced in us – and we can extend that balance out into the world, becoming an influence and a resource to others seeking wisdom. Today let us be the Sophia of God living and working for the good of all.

MARCH 2 – UNDERSTANDING – I am understanding. I understand that Goddess stands under all things. She stands under all things and is totally involved in all things. All seeming disorder is brought into divine order. My love for life is my love for Goddess. The Jewish mystics call this understanding Binah. It is a knowing that comes from nursing at the breast of Sophia (wisdom of God). An early Kabbalist says: "No Creature can contemplate the wondrous paths of Wisdom except one who sucks from It". This is meditation through nursing, not through knowing. A sense of being fed by the Goddess herself is what we seek today. So one who feels the love of Mother creation, who has been nourished by the presence of of this feminine aspect of God. Who feels the same relationship as infant to mother is he/she who will ultimately come to true understanding. Today, let's relax into this idea. The universe is feeding us right now... we are receiving all that we have need of and more. We are nourished and maintained by the great Mother.

MARCH 3 – PARENT – I am a child of the Mother. God is Father and Mother. God is not only fatherly; God is also the mother who lifts her beloved child from the ground to her knee. The all-ness of God is like the folds of a mother's garments wherein the child finds a home and lays its head on the maternal breast. We are indeed surrounded by the roundness of divine compassion. God is truly Father, but also Mother...and we all are enclosed...God is our true Mother in whom we are endlessly carried and out of whom we will never come. Father and Mother of Nature, of the world, of the whole of creation. All things flow out of God to work for goodwill. Take a moment now to feel the joy of God, the delight that God feels in being our Mother. Then feel the security and the comfort of having this ultimate parent. We are being loved and cared for in every moment of every day.

MARCH 4 – UNITY – I am unified. I see the unity of all things in the feminine face of God. The Goddess manifests Herself in the Unity of all life. The land is the symbol of her body, she expresses in water and stone, in tomb and cave, in animals and birds, snakes and fish, hills, trees and flowers. She is the embodiment of all that is sacred in the earth. The goddess is the living mystery in me. Her spirit heals and harmonizes the disparate conditions in my mind and body. Her guidance leads to healing and harmony in all my relationships. I am intimately involved in the flow of life, connected to and part of all other living things. The power of the Divine feminine lives in my intuition. Today I will listen to that feminine voice in my heart.

MARCH 5 – AWARE – I am aware of God. Sometimes I find myself thinking of God as a person. I really know that God is much more than some giant guy in the sky, but I have a game that I play with Him…I occasionally see Her as the Supreme Person, the one who knows everything, as She who is the oldest, who is the Controller, as He who is the smallest and larger than the largest. He who is the Great Maintenance Man. She who is beyond material conception, who is inconceivable, and who is somehow still a person – Luminous like the sun and transcendent – beyond this material nature and still the totality of this material nature. A person who is me and you and everyone else, but also beyond what we in this form can be. When I know you, I know God. I just remember that I cannot know the all of God and that's OK today. I know the name of God is my name, I know the name of God is your name, and I also know that the name of God is unknowable. It is a glorious contradiction and somehow it is a comfort to me.

MARCH 6 – POTENT – I am sacred. My sexuality is sacred. God is present in my sexuality. It cannot be otherwise. The potent power of the universe dwells in my loins. From prehistoric times we have celebrated fertility, potency, abundance and multiplication. This celebration is the joy we take in the perpetuation of life and the preservation of life forces. Seasonal awareness grows in me, I am connected to the ebb and flow of life. I am comfortable with the cycle of life…birth, growth, harvest, death, rebirth…all occur in me and all around me. My sexuality is directly linked to this cycle of life, even if my orientation is not procreative. The forces that are at play in me are creative and I revel in them. There is great power in passion, I do not deny it or put it aside but I do not allow it to run my life. I consecrate it.

MARCH 7 – ENERGIZED – I am energized. I awaken to the energy of creation. My sexual energy is the sacred energy of of creation. As the Zohar says. "Any image that does not embrace male and female is not a high and true image. Come and see: The blessed Holy One does not place his abode in any place where male and female are not found together. Blessings are found only in a place where male and female are found, a human being is only called Adam when male and female are one." When male and female are one the presence of Shekinah is generated. This is the Jewish name for the energy of creation. Hence the birth of Moses: "Shekinah was present on their bed and their desire joined with her. Therefore, Shekinah never left the son they engendered, confirming what is written: "make yourselves holy and you will be holy. Their desire focused on joining Shekinah; so Shekinah joined in the very act they were engaged in. Shekinah is present wherever two or more are gathered together. The balance of male and female energies exemplified by the Christ in me. Physical equipment aside, male and female are balanced in me and in my partnership.

MARCH 8 – ATTRACTION – I am attracted to creation. The attraction I feel is God calling to herself. Sexual attraction is life yearning to extend more of itself. This yearning is for the sake of creation. This creation is not necessarily just the creation of new bodies. There is also a great love to be created, which goes on to bless everyone. Sexual union for the sake of heaven is holy and pure. Union of mankind, when it is right, is the secret of civilization. What makes it right is becoming a conscious partner with God in the act of creation. Whereas we may have always hoped that God wasn't looking, God is in the midst and the mix of it. This is the secret meaning of the sayings of the sages: "When a man unites with his mate in holiness, the divine presence is between them." This is the inspiration of the holy spirit and should never be denigrated. Our attractions are good and they are from Creation.

MARCH 9 – SINGING – I am a song of life. The Song of Songs plays in my soul. The Hebrew Bible's "Song of Songs" is an ode to the interconnectedness of life. "O for his arms around me, beneath me and above!" Has the imagery of being surrounded and enfolded in Love? The imagery that follows links this obvious sexual energy to the wilderness and the wildlife that dwells there. Today I remember that the greening of spring will soon be all around me and also in my body, mind and soul. I revel in the rising energy tide of the season. I am filled with a sense of wonder at the beauty and diversity of God's creation. I appreciate each and every flower, field, person and animal, seeing something unique that was created by God. I am filled with the power of awe and I sing my thanks for my place in creation.

MARCH 10 – FREE – I am free from repression. I do not allow old, negative thinking about sex to cause needless shame. I let go of these old ideas. I am a perfect child of God and the yearnings of my body are in harmony with Creation. I look beyond any seeming barriers, keeping an open mind and my thoughts focused on Love. I am not bound by a particular lifestyle. I have the strength of mind and the faith to step out, onward and upward to my freedom. Through my prayers, I am aware of the presence of God – my source of strength. I am no longer willing to be a victim of my own habitual negative thinking or the opinions of others. I am able to move forward because I am free and unlimited through God's spirit within me. As long as no one is harmed, I can allow my sexual energy to express freely.

MARCH 11 – HARMONIOUS --- I am harmonious. Nature and Grace are in harmony with me. The physical energy of my body and the spiritual energy of my soul are in harmony. It is only my thoughts of separation that makes this seem not so. My body is part of creation…my spirit is part of creation; they cannot be separate. I may think that my spirit is in disagreement with my body and this creates an invisible but seemingly impenetrable wall, it creates division in me. This wall is coming down today as I decide for harmony. I am working to renew and restore harmony of body, mind and spirit. I invite the wisdom and love of God to shape my thoughts and actions. Harmony works wonders within me, blessing me with peace of mind. Harmony will prevail even in the most difficult times as I acknowledge the presence of God in the midst of me. All of my fragments are united in divine harmony.

MARCH 12 – PARTICIPATION – I am a participant in life. I participate in and take joy in life. I do not just sit on the sidelines and watch as time goes by. I am mindful and aware of what goes on around me but I am not just a spectator. I am involved in the ongoing unfoldment of the universe. My involvement starts with taking joy in every part of living. I find golden moments in each day as I connect intimately with Creation. I revel in the creative energy in my body, mind and spirit. I do not deny the physical, I do not denigrate the mental, and I do not ignore the spiritual. I move past any seeming limitations of the past and immerse myself fully in the present. I realize my own sacredness and my sacred link to all life. I realize that I am on holy ground, right now. I experience oneness with God and therefore with everything in my life. Today I participate in life…and it is a joy.

MARCH 13 – FAMILY – I am part of a family. God is my divine parent. God is creator and loving parent to me, to all others and to the universe. God is not mad at us. He is not punishing us. We are being loved every moment. We can trust God to care for the world. Today, release any burden we may have been carrying concerning the welfare of the world. We may have been worried about war or the economy or just the general state of affairs, but we remind ourselves that God is everywhere present. The Spirit of creation is moving in and through all life. Sometimes our brothers and sisters have chosen to ignore the presence of God within them and then through fear and the misuse of free will have seemingly caused problems for us or others. Again, we remind ourselves that the presence of the Divine is always offering good to us all. All we have to do is to turn our attention to it. Today, know that God is caring for all of creation. So, let go and trust God, our divine parent, to care for the world.

MARCH 14 – INNOCENT – I am innocent. As a child of God, I am innocent. God is not holding anything against me. God does not forgive me, because He was never upset with me. So, I forgive myself my mistakes. I am guiltless, the mistakes that I have made are just that, mistakes, and they can be corrected. The errors of yesterday can be healed with a generous application of love today. In the past I may have held onto feelings of guilt and remorse because I thought that I needed to be held to account for my many shortcomings. I may have felt that I deserved to be punished, but I now know that I have suffered enough. Today, I understand that being accountable means that I first take responsibility for my actions, then I do what is necessary to repair the harm and finally I release myself from the bondage of guilt. Holding to guilt is a sure way to hold on to old patterns. It sets me up for repeating the same mistakes over and over again. So, today, I forgive myself my mistakes and I move on, opening the way for new experiences.

MARCH 15 – JOY – I am filled with joy. The presence of God in me is Joy. It is not something we go out and buy on the time payment plan. It is not a new car or a new house or a new set of clothes. Joy is a state of being. It is the state of knowing God and fearing no more. The bliss of this knowing is all-pervading. It is the attraction between husband and wife, parents and children, creature and creature, God and man. It is the infinite love of Creation pouring itself out into our being all the time. It fills us with laughter that sometimes comes bubbling out at seemingly inappropriate moments. This laughter is the expression of a playful spirit. Sometimes, our bliss is overshadowed by negative obsession, but not today...that darkness is cleansed by the power of happiness. There are songs and shouts of joy in the temple of the heart. Bliss is our state and our being.

MARCH 16 – FEARLESS – I am fearless. Understanding that God is love, I have nothing to fear. I am following a path that leads from fear to courage to fearlessness. When fear shows itself, I act in spite of it. I do not allow superstitions of the past interfere with my living today. In this way the fear fades and eventually comes no more. I am inspired by those who live fearlessly and I emulate them in my approach to life. Therefore, I can be a beacon and a help to those who are caught up in fear. Through openness I have gained a new perspective on life. I follow the principles of love to the best of my ability. I have faith in those close to me; I know that they believe in me and I believe in them. I keep my thoughts centered on living in the moment. I remember the adage: "There are only two things in life: love and fear, and fear is just a lie I tell myself." So I will live in love where there is no fear.

MARCH 17 – GIFT – I am giving. I have no fear of lack, so I am free in my giving. I give to life and life gives to me. I am the power of love expressing as me in life. I carry my own weight, doing the things that need to be done by me, but I am unafraid to ask for help when I need it. In this way I become part of the great flow of good in the universe. As I give freely without concern, I am provided for without effort. What may appear to be difficult is easily accomplished by me when I act from love. However, I also have learned to give wisely from inner guidance. Sometimes I must restrain my generosity if it appears that my help may actually allow someone to become stuck in dependence, I would do better to teach interdependence. I trust the voice for God to direct me in my giving, knowing that the same voice is directing even more good my way.

MARCH 18 – SPIRITUAL – I am spiritual. The beauty of God inspires me. I begin my day by becoming aware of the presence of God. This presence shines forth from everything in my world. I do not have to search for someone or something to fill any seeming emptiness in me. My soul will be satisfied when I turn my attention to the beauty of God. That beauty is within and all around me. In silence, I receive deep inspiration…insight into my own inner workings and the inner workings of the world. Great blessings come to me in the form of divine ideas that I can in turn pass on to others. My spirit is filled with an inspiration that cannot be hidden, it shines forth from me and spreads good to all who come into contact with me. I am inspired to be creative, inspired to bring even more beauty to life. As a result, overflowing abundance comes into my life. The beauty of God inspires me to greatness.

MARCH 19 – SPIRIT – I am spirit. God is spirit. First and foremost, I am spirit. It is easy to identify myself with my body, but I must remember that my body is a temporary phenomenon. It is neutral host which can be symbol for love or for fear. The body can be filled with the strength of spirit. Through spirit I am whole and free. I know that wholeness means that I am connected with all spirit which means that I am connected with all others, and with God. Through the strength of spirit, I overcome all sense of separation and any negative habits that my body or my mind may become involved in. I cannot be limited by anyone or anything. I release all negativity and welcome God's will for me. I express freedom of Spirit and soar to new heights of fulfillment.

MARCH 20 – OPEN-MINDED – I am open-minded. I am open to the possibilities of daily life. I am a thought in the mind of God, so I will empty my mind and be receptive to God's plan for me. From the crucible of that potential, I create my world. From the Tao te Ching: "Empty your mind of all thoughts, let your heart be at peace. Watch the turmoil of beings, but contemplate their return. Each separate being in the universe returns to the common source. Returning to the source is serenity." So, I see my brother being healed from the emptiness within himself; I see myself being made whole from the divine space in me. From this serene place I allow my dreams to come forth. I open my mind and heart and listen to the inspiration that God is always pouring out to me. Then I use my imagination to peruse all of the divine possibilities. Since all possibilities exist in this potential, I can decide what I want to bring forth. What I bring forth from this place of pure potential is my creation, my co-creation with God. All of this possibility fills me with awe and an awareness of what could be.

MARCH 21 – BEGIN – I am beginning. Today is a new beginning. The first full day of Spring...this is a new beginning. I am filled with the creative spirit of God and I use this spirit to shape my life. The joy of new life is stirring underfoot. This joy is stirring all around me; it is stirring within me. I resolve to think and act in ways that encourage health and peace and fulfillment. Today I am making a commitment to a beginning, but I also realize that every day holds perfect potential. Today I decide to act, to pursue my goals. My meditation connects me with divine mind. Creation is guiding me to the fulfillment of my dreams, but I must take the action. I am responsible for moving my goals from formlessness to form; from idea to manifestation. This new life in me, the stirring of spring, promises a full harvest of Joy.

MARCH 22 – PROTECTION – God is my protection. I am confident in the protection of God. As long as I practice the presence of God, as long as I know that God is always with me, my confidence abounds. I understand that alone I am powerless to accomplish the desires of my heart. Alone, in ego, I have a hard time making a right decision. However, when I surrender to Spirit, I am filled with confidence. A renewed energy builds in me and my enthusiasm overflows. I am able to consider a wide range of objectives and I know that with God, I can achieve any of them. I have nothing to fear. The power of creation will work through me to accomplish great and amazing things. With faith in God and confidence in myself, I see that all things are possible.

MARCH 23 – CHOSEN – I am choosing. I am the light of world. It is almost scary to consider what this means. It may seem like ego talking, but really it was Jesus who said: "You are the light of the world" Matthew 5:14. I see the light of God making Itself evident in my life. I am going to take time to remind myself and others of the good news that we are chosen, that we are the light of the world. I see us all united in joy and thanksgiving. I have been actively developing strong belief in the omnipresence of good in the world and I am filled with an overflowing joy. This happiness flows out from me as light. No matter how dark things seem to be, a ray of hope always breaks through and shines before me, showing me the way. The light of God shining through me and others is a beacon guiding my steps. Today I will be focused and ever aware that I am chosen to shine.

MARCH 24 – PRACTICE – I am faithful. My practice activates my faith. Thich Naht Hanh points out: "It is not a matter of faith; it is a matter of practice" I choose a method, it is not that important what method it is…I repeat it, I set aside time at the beginning of the day and possibly at the end of the day…I make it my custom, I make the repetition my custom and my companion taking it with me into my everyday affairs…I become skilled, I can activate it at any time and under any circumstances. It is through this routine that practice activates faith. My practice is the path to true vision and faith is the perceiving power. The quality of my meditative practice impacts how I see life. The practice may be stopping, calming and looking deeply; stopping…stop activity for some period of time, sit quietly not doing anything; calming…relax the body and calm the mind; looking deeply…look past appearance, get under the surface. I am mindful, immersed in the present moment, I can see and listen deeply.

MARCH 25 – VISION – I am visionary. Spiritual vision reveals God's Will for us. Vision shows us that which can be. Vision proceeds from formlessness into form. Our dreams can show us our potential, our purpose and our mission. These dreams are God's gentle guidance, leading us in the right direction. Others are also receiving their own guidance and we do not have to be concerned about telling them what to do. We are all directly connected to the mind of Creation and communication comes to us in the still small voice, a strong, persistent knowing or perhaps even a full blown vision. This seeing is so powerful that it fills us with the energy to accomplish great things. As we go about our day, we keep our vision in front of us. As we move toward the higher goal, we are in harmony with God's will.

MARCH 26 – ATTENTION – I am paying attention. I give my attention to life. Today, I will approach my tasks with exuberance, I am excited about life and I expect the best. I stay in this day, I live in the moment and focus on the now. This is mindfulness. As I sit quietly preparing for the tasks of the day, I am totally aware of my surroundings and not just aware but immersed in them. I realize my ultimate oneness with all things. As I get up and begin to move, I feel my body, I feel the ground beneath my feet, I am aware of the air through which I pass. If I eat, I taste every bite, I revel in each morsel. When I drink I notice my thirst and everything about the water; the coolness, the texture, the volume, the quenching. As I meet people, I am intimately aware of them. I feel them as much as see them, I honor their presence, and I cherish their company. I give my attention to what they are saying to me; I hear the words but more importantly I understand the meanings both the obvious and the hidden. This mindfulness allows me to fully and consciously join with all of creation. I express the joy of God and my joy then mixes with the joy of others around me and around the world.

MARCH 27 – UNAFRAID – I am unafraid. Today I will have an inner victory. As my daily practice deepens, my hunger for truth increases. When fear show itself as feelings like disappointment, embarrassment, irritation, resentment, anger, and jealousy it is clear that I am holding back. I may feel like collapsing and backing away, instead I perk up and lean in. I will hold back no longer. I am in control of my inner world. I decide how I will act on feelings. Through accepting responsibility for my life, I am strong. I surrender to the creative power within me and begin to direct that power, first on the inside and then on the outside. I am mindful enough to embrace fear and the anger that comes from it, giving it a loving transformation. This embrace, this love is my inner victory and it gives me the courage to engage in the outer.

MARCH 28 – DELIGHT – I am filled with delight. Looking up the word joy in the dictionary, one of the definitions is delight. That's a good word. It implies that I know that great good is coming to me. I am filled with a sense of well-being. I know that all of the love in the universe is mine to give and to receive. This is good fortune, indeed… it fuels my sense of possibilities. This is the opposite of the feeling of disillusionment. The word right above joy in the dictionary is "jowly". It means having marked jowls; full and saggy flesh about the lower cheeks and jaw area…as in an elderly man with a disillusioned face. Reading this now, picturing jowly-ness if that is a word…oh, it's not… but it gives me a kick…and some small delight. Looking in the mirror I notice that I, myself, have become jowly! The humor of creation is the gift of joy and that gift is mine.

MARCH 29 – SMILE – I am smiling. God fills my soul with gladness. The smile on my face shows that I am enjoying the moment, but the spark of life in my eyes is evident to everyone that I am full of the Spirit of joy. This joy does not come from others; it cannot be infused by the situation of the moment. It is on the inside; it is the elation that comes from my relationship with Spirit. No matter what happens to me or around me, I stay the course. I am upbeat and positive. I know that I can do all things and weather all storms because I have a buoy of happiness that is constantly uplifting me. Creation is the source of my gladness. My life is rich and growing richer because that spirit is being expressed through me. Today I am the harbinger of joy, it comes with me and moves out to embrace the others in my life. My smile is the happy introduction, but my eyes are the genuine messengers, delivering love and directly from my joy-filled soul.

MARCH 30 – CHALLENGES – I am joyful. I know true joy in the midst of suffering. Even when I feel at a low emotional point, I can pick myself and renew my appreciation of life. It would be foolish to believe that we will never be touched by pain and suffering. Joy is not the opposite of suffering and pain – joy is what sees me through them both. I can reclaim my joy be recognizing how much God has blessed me. Acknowledging the presence of the Divine, I am able to give thanks and to know that somewhere in this seeming problem is a blessing. Again, I remind myself of Jacob wrestling with his angel all night long, dislocated hip and all…in the end he got his blessing and his answer. In the midst of any trouble I can remember to give thanks for life. I embrace the challenge, giving it love and knowing that it is indeed a blessing in disguise. I say thank you God for this gift, even though I am still wondering what it is good for… The spirit will uplift me, as I continue to recognize the presence of God in my life. Today I will be happy in the midst of trouble, joyous in the midst of pain and I will come out the other end with a blessing.

MARCH 31 – HEALING – I am healed. The beauty of Creation heals me. I am healed by the love of God. All healing comes directly from communion with Creation. Sometimes a doctor may facilitate the process but only God heals. Becoming aware of and in awe of the beauty of creation, fills me with love which in turn heals my mind and body. Knowing that I am one with this beauty restores me to sanity, health and wholeness. The rose outside my window opens its heart and gives the world its beauty. It feels the encouragement of the sun's light upon its being. In this light it feels the love of God and opens unto it. Today, I will be like the rose opening up to the light of God. I will be healed and I will help heal others through my own unfoldment.

APRIL

Love Eases

Hard edge
Between,
Softened
Then eased.
Rocky madness
Smoothed in
The flow.
Where fear
Had distressed
Now love eases.

APRIL 1 – NOT FOOLED – I am making quality choices. I am not fooled by imitations. Today I do not waste time, energy or resources on false idols. I want the genuine article in my life. I am not interested in cheap imitations. I will not settle for less the real thing. I surround myself with quality. I would rather eat a little bit of great food, than a whole trough of buffet garbage. My furniture will be well crafted and designed, it will last me a life-time and then I will pass it on to someone else. When I buy new clothes, I will buy only that which excites and inspires me. If I can only afford something less than that, I will consider waiting until I can get what I really want. I love and appreciate the creativity that people have put into making things of great beauty. I know that Creation is speaking through their art and their craft. I am not fooled by imitations and I don't want them.

APRIL 2 – UNFOLDING – I am unfolding. Infinite beauty is unfolding all around me. The universe exploding from a tiny pin-prick of light into a great flower of expansion can be a symbol of the extension of love or it can be a source of further separation. Infinite beauty is unfolding all around us and within us. Out of seeming chaos Spirit orders all life. We connect to that order through the power of God's presence in us. We can tap into the same inexhaustible source of divine energy that fuels the unfolding universe. We, too, are filled with the divine power to create beauty. The creative power of God is unfolding through us as the life we live. How we live life is a statement worship. Today let will unfold and extend ourselves in love.

APRIL 3 – RESOURCE – I am resourceful. We are a resource in preserving beauty. If we release all obsession for power over others, if we let go of control and allow the creativity of God to come forth in all our interactions with the world we become assets to our communities. We are concerned with preserving and promoting the beauty and grandeur of the planet. We are protectors of natural beauty and champions of artistic beauty. Fear and a sense of separation has brought the world to the brink of disaster. Let's do all that we can to facilitate harmony and understanding. We can conserve resources and pay attention to what we consume and how we dispose of the waste. In familial situations teach conservation and appreciation of beauty, in the community we stay involved in the arts and the ecology. Truly, we become enlightened by a love for and an appreciation of beauty. Our voice can be heard nationally and worldwide, because it is the combined voice of judgement and love, in other words wisdom.

APRIL 4 – INSPIRATION – I am inspired. The beauty of God inspires me. I begin my day by becoming aware of the divine presence. This presence shines forth from everything in my world. I do not have to search for someone or something to fill any seeming emptiness in me. My soul will be satisfied when I turn my attention to the beauty of life. That beauty is within and all around me. In silence, I receive deep inspiration…insight into my own inner workings and the inner workings of the world. Great blessings come to me in the form of divine ideas that I can in turn pass on to others. My spirit is filled with an inspiration that cannot be hidden, it shines forth from me and spreads good to all who come into contact with me. I am inspired to be creative, inspired to bring even more beauty to life. As a result, overflowing abundance comes into my life. The beauty of God inspires me to greatness.

APRIL 5 – APPRECIATION – I am filled with appreciation for all the beautiful things. To truly appreciate the beauty all around us is to be open and receptive. We must continually practice this openness. Hafiz says: "God's beauty has split me wide open. Throw Hafiz on a scale, wrap me in cloth, bring me home, lift a piece of my knowledge to your lips so I can melt inside of you and sing". When we allow ourselves to be open, actually to be opened by the wonderful creation all around us we become the heralds of love and joy and peace. Our enlightened presence makes others more aware and more open to the beauty of life. We continue to look for ways to free our brothers and sisters from the bondage of the mundane. Again Hafiz: "The small man builds cages for everyone he knows. While the sage, who has to duck his head when the moon is low, keeps dropping keys all night long for the beautiful rowdy prisoners." Today I appreciate the unexpected beauty in life and keep myself open to it.

APRIL 6 – REQUIREMENT – I am surrounded by beauty. I require, not acquire, beauty. I can never own beauty, it is an essence that cannot be held. To surround oneself with beauty is a noble thing. To be able to appreciate quality, craft and art are essential in the recognition creativity flowing from the people around us. It is not vain to wish to clothe oneself with finery. To feel the perfection of the fabric, to revel in the cut is part of appreciating the Good. Those who make these fine garments are living out their talent through the making of the clothes. To decorate the house or office with fine art is to worship God. To bring beauty to life and to bring this life into our surroundings is to become part of the flow of creation. However, to want to own these things, to want to collect and acquire because someone else may be impressed is counter-productive. We cannot own beauty, we can only care for it, be stewards of it. When we are finished with it we should immediately send it on to someone else's care. Today, I will allow beauty to flow through my life and my living.

APRIL 7 – RESURRECTED – I am rising. He has risen! This is the Easter cry throughout the world each year. Today we consider our resurrection day. Let this be the thought for ourselves this day…we have risen, we have risen from the ashes…we have overcome the material world…we are son and heir to the kingdom of God. Whatever the past has held for us we are released from it today. We will not bear that burden any longer. We may have hoisted ourselves up onto this cross and allowed ourselves to be nailed to it. Well, the sacrifice is over…we can get down right now. We need longer be victim to the egos of others or to our own. We will rise above any seeming adversity and live life anew…Today is resurrection day and we are rising.

APRIL 8 – LIVE – I am letting go to live. We let go and live. We have all heard let go and let God, live and let live…today let's put these two ideas together…let go and live. Release all of the regrets and resentments of the past and start living today. Let go of all need to control others and start living today. Let's live every moment of this day, reveling in the joy and also staying with any suffering that might come our way. We are aware of happiness and suffering, we accept both but cling to neither. We let go of any need to judge, to hold grievance, or debt. Just be, right now. And when it is time we can do as Meister Eckhart instructs, let go and die. His concept of dying was letting go…He knew that death and rebirth go together. He knew that letting go leads to breakthrough…we know that letting go in life leads to breakthroughs in living and just as surely letting go in death leads to breakthrough into rebirth. Today, we let go and live.

APRIL 9 – UNDIVIDED – I am undivided. We are immersed in life and life breaks through as us. We can see ourselves as waves in the great sea of life. We move with the tides, for hundreds and thousands of miles we move onward drawn by unseen forces to some far off beach. We are waves of life and we cannot be apart from the sea of life. We cannot be divided. We move and move and gather energy until finally we crash onto that beach, but this is not the end... we seem to empty on to the beach but very quickly we are pulled back into the sea, returning to our source. Nothing is ever lost. No warmth is lost in the universe. No beauty is lost; no life is lost. We are still in life and life still breaks through as us; life cannot be divided.

APRIL 10 – CELEBRATION – I am celebrating. Today we celebrate life. We give thanks for the good that has come to me and focus on relieving the suffering of others. Our life is full and our compassion is great. When we are thankful for what we have, we are moved to give freely. We understand and embrace the seeming contradiction of the phrase "We keep what we have by giving it away." As we give, Creation prospers us each day in myriad ways. We celebrate the cool breeze, the gentle rain, and the refreshing fragrance of spring. Good continues to come to us and move through us. Let us look for ways to be a blessing to others, celebrating life by sharing it to the utmost.

APRIL 11 – COMPASSION – I am compassionate. Let us be compassionate in all of our dealings with others today. We have a sympathetic consciousness of others. When others suffer, we feel distress and we naturally want to alleviate that suffering. Remembering the words of the Buddha: "Fill your mind with compassion!". Knowing the interrelatedness of all life and the compassion that grows out of that knowing prepares us for a life of service. Our response to the interconnectivity of creation is to give that which we have to give. As we sit quietly and consider our one-ness with the universe, it is possible to have an awakening of the spirit. Let us continue to give compassionate service wherever we can. Surely this will hasten our enlightenment.

APRIL 12 – BREATH – I am breathing. Today let us allow the breath to guide us in all of interactions with the world. As we keep our attention on and follow the breath we are able to look deeply into life. Attending to the breath the mind becomes a tool in the removal of the suffering that is present in all of us. We become calm and see through to the truth...all suffering comes from a sense of separation, a sense of isolation. In calmness we return to one-ness and thus alleviate our own suffering. As we look still deeper we see that all those who may have harmed us in any way whatsoever are also suffering from this fear of being alone. We clearly see that anyone who has made us suffer is suffering themselves. Compassion leads to understanding and forgiveness. As we breathe in the love of forgiveness and breathe out the light of understanding we alleviate suffering everywhere.

APRIL 13 – HEART – I am open-hearted. I open my heart and allow the love of God to flow. The love of God flows from my heart and returns to flow into my heart. My heart is a pump, delivering not just blood around my body but also delivering compassion to myself and to others. Today I truly care about people, even people who are fearful, angry, jealous, overpowered by addiction, arrogant, proud, miserly, selfish…My heart filters out any fear of finding these unattractive things in myself and it filters out my judgements of people who exhibit them as well. I no longer have to be afraid of pain, I can open my heart and allow myself to feel my own suffering and the suffering of others. The pain softens and purifies me and then makes me more loving and kind. I do not cling to pain, but rather experience it, bless it, and send it on its way…

APRIL 14 – CALM – I am calm. I release all need for revenge or retribution. I give understanding and empathy and I receive compassion. I see myself as totally nonviolent and non-aggressive. I empty myself of all fear, allowing for the possibility of connecting with unconditional openness. From this loving foundation I can build a new life and a new world. A quiet wisdom envelops me and true knowledge displays itself to me. This is my birthright as a child of Creation, divine wisdom itself. Calm and centered, I have no intention of causing harm...I am mindful of causing no harm...a sense of clear seeing descends upon me...I have respect and compassion for all that I perceive...this mindfulness is the ground of understanding and refraining from harm is the path of compassion.

APRIL 15 – TREASURE – I am. Where your treasure is so shall your heart be also…today, release all the desires of the ego and suffering is alleviated…bliss comes from realizing the desires of the heart. There is a great goodness in the midst of you…your talents and abilities are gifts that are calling out for expression. When you give these gifts to the world they become a treasure…and you become a treasure. This is the work of the compassionate seeker, to strive to bring these inner riches to others. Some would confuse you saying this pursuit would be impractical…do not listen to their fearful words…Let the glory of God speak through you and your works. Remember the words of Jesus "Do not worry about what you will wear or what you will eat" …Give your treasure to life and life will give an even greater treasure to you.

APRIL 16 – LISTEN – I am listening. Let us pay attention to the spirit's loving instruction. Soon we will see others not as object but as subject. Our fellows are subject to all of the feelings, wants and needs that we may be subject to. Trusting the loving spirit within, we seek first to understand and then to be understood. In the past we may have overlooked the true meaning in another's words or actions simply because we were seeing them as some object of my desire. If we do not understand it is very difficult to be understood. In our relationships at home, work or in the community let us stop seeing others as means to an end. We can begin by noticing that they are spiritual beings just like us. We can be a better friend, confidants and lovers when we allow the truth of our common origin to direct us. We focus on the others in our life, looking and listening with love. We need no longer fear misunderstanding. We are inspired to do and say the right things at just the right time.

APRIL 17 – OPEN – I am open and honest in my relationships. I have no need to control the behavior of anyone else. I radiate love and understanding. As I keep an open heart and an open mind I am sensitive to the needs of others and especially so with my partner and I know when to bring things out into the open. I pay close attention to what is being communicated to me and I stay open to new ideas. I understand that God speaks to and through everyone, I just have to be willing to hear. As I share openly I become more relaxed and am able to listen deeply so that I gain a new perspective. I am open and receptive to the wants and needs of my partner and that results in my partner being open and receptive to what I have to share.

APRIL 18 – REAL – I am real. Let us take a chance and be "real" with the one person that we feel closest to. As we practice with this person, we can make progress in being genuine. We have become accustomed to misrepresenting ourselves. The need for the acceptance and approval of others has driven a self-defeating behavior. Our best hope for true intimacy is to let go of all the false images we have been holding and projecting out to others. Today, we take a chance with someone we we can trust. Let us relax into the breath and then just allow our real self to come forth. At our core we are pure and loving spirit, so let us allow that spirit to come forth.

APRIL 19 – HUMAN – I am human. Today I accept my humanity. I release any false sense of self and replace it with true self-knowledge. Being human does not mean being less than divine. Accepting my humanity is part of humility: knowing who I am and not trying to act like something else. Today I know that I am a spiritual being, I am a thinking being, and I am a sexual being. I am part of the larger Creation. I am child of creation and creation is interested in the physical, the mental and the physical. Old ideas of sexuality and sin do not apply to me or anyone else. I am free to express my humanity and its accompanying sexuality any way that does not cause suffering to myself or others. Everyone else is also free to do the same. I need feel no shame or guilt over these natural attributes. I understand and appreciate that I am precious in the sight of God as I am and as I do. I can be honest and forthright in all my dealings because I am confident in the power that is within me.

APRIL 20 – STRONG – I am strong. With each breath I am filled with inner strength. There is a strength in me, it seems to live in the very center of my body, but it is actually in the middle of my mind, and at the core of my spirit. As I walk, I feel myself being pulled from my center. I glide effortlessly through life. All of my physical movement begins from this spot, this chakra, this chi. I breathe from my center, I allow my diaphragm to expand and fill with air. As I inhale, I feel myself being filled with strength. As I exhale, I freely breathe out power to others. I inhale power from creation, I exhale strength to creation. I am breathing spirit. I focus on the flow. There is no need to conserve the air, I inhale and exhale freely and fully. There is no loss, only greater good for everything. With each breath I am filled with inner strength.

APRIL 21 – GENTLE – I am gentle. I forgive rage. I understand that rage is frustration. Previously, I may have been plagued with this disorder, but today I am able to forgive. I do not allow my own rage or the rage of others to contaminate me. I forgive the person who has caused me the most discomfort…myself. I forgive whatever appearance of harm that others may have put upon me. I know that I can be gentle, but strong. I have no need to make an aggressive show of strength. If I am in danger, I move quickly and easily out of harm's way. I can be gentle, but firm in my position. I am like the aikido master, I strike no blows, nor take offensive action, yet I am untouched by injury. I am gentle and calm, and I let the energy of any attack move over me without harm.

APRIL 22 – UNAFRAID – I am unafraid. I forgive fear. I am aware that fear is the cause and justification of almost all harm done by one to another. I am not afraid...I tap into this great well of power that is within me and I cannot be hurt. I allow any fear I feel to be healed and turned into love. I do not feel separate or apart from, rather I am one with creation. There may be many things that I do not agree with, but I refuse to be against anyone or anything. I remember Jesus' words "resist not evil". I will work for the positive unfoldment of good, I will not waste my energy fighting "evil". I choose to give my life force to the opposite positive thing rather than getting myself all stirred up with righteous indignation. I forgive fear, mine own and everyone else's.

APRIL 23 – TRANSFORMATION – I am transformed. I transform adversity into opportunity. Sometimes this idea might appear to be a cliché, regardless, it is the truth. It is apparent to me that within every problem there is a solution. Rather than angrily focusing on the negative effects, I look for the presence of spirit in every seeming difficulty. I am focused on the essence and the source. I can transform my life because I understand cause and effect. I am aware of the link between thoughts and actions, between actions and consequences…I can change my thinking and therefore change outcomes. I can change my mind and change my life.

APRIL 24 – REPRESENTATION – I am representing good. I stand for the good. I am a representation of creation, acting as me and through me. I stand for good, I will not stand for lack and fear. I will not stand for greed and power mongering. I speak out for the good of community. I speak out for equality of all people. I speak out for the common welfare. But I will not be against anything. I am for good. I am for the best. I am for the love of God. I am a representation and a representative of the Divine. Sometimes it may seem that some evil is a danger, when this happens, I work for the opposite good thing. I do not have to fear any seeming evil thing because I am one with God.

APRIL 25 – AUTHENTIC – I am authentic. We have authentic power. The power in us is Divine. It is for creation. The power in us is for love and the extension of more love. The power in us builds the life that we want. It allows us to design life and then put it together as we will. We understand that the life we have now is the life we have co-created. If something in life is not to our liking, we need to figure out why we have chosen it. We are choosing our lives in many ways great and small; getting some kind of payoff, some kind of reward for the way we are living. We have the ability to choose what we want in life. We can change our mind right now and begin to create the life and circumstances which we truly desire. This power we yield is over and above some personal ego power, it is the image and likeness of God in us, it is the essence of creation.

APRIL 26 – SHARED – I am sharing. I share power with others. I do not pursue power over others. I see clearly that the need to exert control over others is futile, it can never be satisfied and just continually feeds itself with more need. There will never be enough. I see that when I act in concert with others, all of our power grows. I know that when I share the strength that I have, it is multiplied. In reality we all share the strength of Creation. All other power is illusion, a fantasy that tries to impose negative consequences on my community and on the world. Sharing, this is what the spiritual warrior does, she lends her strength to all and her strength is increased in the doing. I learn from and emulate the warrior, and thus I become the warrior.

APRIL 27 – GRATEFUL – I am grateful for my life. I am filled with gratitude for life itself. I am thankful for all the gifts that I have been given. My body is healthy and strong. If I am feeling any disease or discomfort it is quickly healed. My mind is quick and responsive. Any confusion that may occur is instantly made clear. My spirit is one with Spirit. If from time to time I feel separate from anyone or anything I remind myself that I am one with my source, I am one with life. I cannot be apart from any other part of life. As I focus on what I have to be thankful for, I know that I am rich and growing richer by the moment. I am grateful for life.

APRIL 28 – FORGIVEN – I am forgiven. From time to time we may feel regret over something that we have done or left undone. When this occurs, we simply forgive ourselves, knowing that God has never held anything against us anyway. We have a great capacity for forgiveness. We need not become involved with recriminations. Let us accept the error and then realize that it can be corrected. Holding on to the past in any way cheats us out of the living moment. If at any point in the day, we find ourselves wishing that we had done a certain thing, or that we had not done another thing…we can stop and let go of this ridiculous idea. Let's get back into the holy instant. We cannot change the past, but we can change what is going on right now. If something can be done about the past event, we do it, otherwise we let go. We are forgiving and forgiven.

APRIL 29 – FORGIVING – I am forgiving. My brother is forgiven. In Spirit we are all innocent. Our practice today is to release anyone who may have harmed us in any way whatsoever. If we are innocent, so then is our sister. We can see everyone as sharing our oneness with God. Let's stop playing the blame game, if we should begin to think "if only that person had not done this or that or the other thing then…everything would have been alright", we will tell ourselves that everything is alright, right now. We hold no one hostage to past any longer; this frees us and all others from the bondage of guilt and shame. There is only the present moment and in that moment we are all share Divine Mind. We do not need to say that the injury was justified, but because the way we remember the injury is incorrect, we can say it did not really happen. We release everyone from guilt and let go of resentment; thereby releasing ourselves. We forgive and forget, and we are all made one.

APRIL 30 – OPTIMISTIC – I am optimistic about life. Pessimism need no longer be part of my life. I understand that the pessimistic view always looks for and expects some negative component, even in the good. This is totally contrary to the way I want to live. Optimism on the other, hand looks for and expects good in all. I align my will with Goodwill, assured that only good can come to me when I am in this receptive state. I do not need any specific event to occur to feel good about my life. I know that no matter what may occur, God's will is always for the best. I am aware of the presence of good in every situation. I am open and receptive to whatever may happen. I use my optimism to prepare me for every blessing and every seeming challenge. Around every corner I will find the opportunity for good waiting me.

MAY

Mothers' Day Rush

Sitting at a corner table alone,
just observing, listening.
The servers hurried, harried,
it's been a long day, the strain
of their smiles noticed only by me.
Grown children trying to make
nice with each other, old conflict
bubbling just below the surface.
Judging each other's gifts,
Mothers graciously accepting those gifts
seeming not to notice that they are all
cheap and purchased without much thought.
Conversation skims across the surface of
banality. Feeling my own loss, tears welling,
I want to warn them, "Wake up,
too soon she will be gone!"

MAY 1 – FEARLESS – I am fearless. Today we release fear. Fear has put us into the very situations which we dread. Fear has prompted us to do that which was not for the common welfare and it has kept us from doing what was. Fear is stimulated from our sense of threat; we feel cut off from safety because we think we are alone. The news of the day and the controversy of the moment encourage that sense of danger. We do not accept information from the media or anyone else that is based in fear. We have nothing to fear. As we pray, our hearts grow stronger. We allow spirit to show us a new way of life. As we follow God's guidance, we get a clear perspective on the day. We see the world through the eyes of love. We can get quiet, practicing meditation and praying throughout the day, allowing the meditations of our hearts to take up residence in life. We have faith in God and in those around us. Our thoughts will be centered on living and enjoying life the way it is. Since we are one with our source, we have nothing to fear.

MAY 2 – HAPPY – I am happy, right now. I am happy with my life just the way it is. Today I practice communion with creation. In everything that I do, I remind myself that I am very holy. My holiness emanates from me to touch everything around me. It is then that I realize that everything and everyone is also very holy. At the essence of life is the divine. Communion means touching the essence, touching the core. I commune with God by finding and touching the divine in all things. When I find the holiness in me is being responded to by the holiness in others, it makes me happy. As I find God, I find undying happiness. I know that God is in everything and I know that everything is in God…and I am happy.

MAY 3 – STRONG-HEART – I am strong. My heart is soft, but strong. My heart speaks to the rest of my body. It balances and aligns the lower chakras with the higher chakras. My heart directs my actions, my heart lends love to my attractions, it soothes bitterness and heals aggression. The heart informs my words and fulfills my potential; my heart inspires my thoughts with love; it blesses my own good fortune and the good fortune of others. I am compassionate and kind, but I am also firm and strong. I am intelligent but also I am intuitive. My heart connects me to both the Mother in me and the Father in me. It allows me to extend love and to receive love. My heart is the fulcrum of my being, it is soft but it is also strong.

MAY 4 – FULFILLED – I am filled with the spirit of creation. If from time to time a sense of emptiness threatens to overwhelm me, I remind myself that I am filled with the spirit of creation. There will never be enough stuff to fill the hole in my ego, even though it continues to tell me that I need more, I know that what I am is enough. As I practice this idea, I begin to feel the truth of it. I am one with and filled with Spirit. The dark place cannot be filled with new toys, it is insatiable. I can be satisfied and quite content with my life and my place in life, when I realize how wonderful it is. I bring the seeming dark place into the light and I am made well. I can speak the truth and recognize that I am filled with the spirit of creation.

MAY 5 – HONEST – I am honest and truthful. Up from my throat and out of my mouth come the words that create my life experience. The throat chakra is the seat of Power. I make a commitment to be honest and truthful in everything that I say. I am also committed to be straight-forward in all of my dealings. I understand the sacredness of the word that proceeds from my mouth. I see the holiness that comes from my intentions and my actions. I will not stand for anything that is counter to my values. I do not need to fight, but I will speak out. I will speak for love, peace, and harmony. I am involved in truth; I do not fool myself or perpetuate deception on anyone else. There is a tremendous burden in dishonesty of any kind, today I lay it down. Today, I am honest and truthful.

MAY 6 – ROADMAP – I am on a mission. My mission is my roadmap. I am not swayed by advertising or any other kind of media exposure. I am not caught up in the pursuit of things. I understand that that race cannot be won. I do not support the consumer economy. I buy what I need and what I truly want. I do not consume for simply for the sake of consumption, that need cannot be met. I allow my mission of stewardship to guide my way. I know that my job is to help care for the planet and all living things. I let my purpose of service light the path in front of me. I am continually satisfied and filled to overflowing by the benefits of giving to life. I release all of the pro-consumerism influence of the media and focus on conservation. I remember my mission and purpose.

MAY 7 – AWARENESS – I am aware. I stay aware of what I am taking in. Today, I will pay particular attention to what I take into my life. I will be mindful of my breath, renewing my gratitude with each one. I will choose healthy food and drink and imbibe reasonable quantities. I will make my purchases based on quality and need. I surround myself with things of beauty, but I understand that these things are only held in trust. I don't have to buy things to feel better. I am a true conservationist, concerned with the state of the world, I do not have to consume more to be fulfilled. I stay aware of what I am taking in.

MAY 8 – COMPLIMENT – I am complimentary. Today I put my focus on the words that issue from my mouth. I make a commitment to be complimentary rather than critical. I stay quiet until I have something positive to say. I keep my own counsel unless I have something constructive to offer. In the past I may have gotten caught up in gossip and generally negative comments about or too others, but today I am all about looking for and reporting the good. I see the Christ in others and I let them know it. I see the good and I describe it. I am aware of the presence of God in me and all around me and I let the word go forth. "Praise and worship" is a phrase that has gotten a bad rap in some circles, but this is exactly what the throat chakra is designed to do. Praise the good and worship (be in awe of) the Presence. Give voice to the power of God that is everywhere present.

MAY 9 – LISTEN – I am listening. I allow others their voice. It is not important for me to stop others from expressing their opinions or observations. Whether I agree with what is said on not I listen with an open mind to the words of others, but I allow the holy spirit to filter all that I hear. In this way, I eliminate the negative and stay receptive to the positive. As I listen, I am taken by new ideas and realize the creativity in others. I am open and receptive to these ideas which in turn inspire me to still other ideas.

MAY 10 – SPEAK – I am speaking. I speak my world into existence. I pay close attention to my words, they are the harbingers of what is to come. If I complain, that which I am protesting may come further into my experience. If I worry aloud, I may help call that which I fear into manifestation. If I express anger and hate, those emotions begin to fill more of my day. Contra-wise when I give praise I am aware of more good, when I stay optimistic I hurry my fortune to me, when I express forgiveness and love my days are blessed. It is well and good to speak out for change, to give voice to justice, but we must be aware of the power of words. Our speech should be well chosen and pointed at solutions rather than just the re-hashing of problems. The power of creation is in my words and I use them wisely.

MAY 11 – COMMUNITY – I am protector of community. Community is the inter-relatedness of all things, not just my neighborhood, my town or my country. I am interested in being a spiritual warrior for the whole community. I want to protect life and revere creation wherever it may be, and of course that means everywhere. I will not be separated from my human brothers and sisters by the politics of a misguided few. I will not forget that I am related to and responsible to all life. I am the one who can enter the dark places of fear and alienation and bring the light of love. I do not need to trumpet my intentions to the world, I can be quiet and full of stealth as bring peace and harmony to the bastions of fear and hate. I accomplish my goal with such grace, that no one realizes that I was even there. I am spiritual warrior and protector of community...the community of all life.

MAY 12 – NEW – I am new. Today is a new day and a fresh start for me. I recognize that I am changing from day to day. Even with the greatest effort the self cannot remain exactly the same from one day to the next. The quality of my spiritual practice, my thoughts, experiences, insights, and revelations effect change in me each day. Every day is a new day and fresh start for me. God does not limit me in any way, all things are possible for me. In the past I may have been frustrated by some things concerning my family, my friends, or my job, but I keep these where they belong, in the past. I know that God is within me and within all others. God is in every situation, helping me and helping others to make a fresh start in life. I know that I can reach any goal and so can everyone else. Today is a new day and a fresh start.

MAY 13 – ORDER – I am calm. We really can be calm in the midst of the storm. Because we know that what seems to be chaotic is really part of divine order, we can relax. We know that no matter what events may appear to be, God is with us and all is well. Divine order is in all things and we just need to turn our awareness to it. We may be very busy, but we can always take the time to get centered and become open to the infinite possibilities that arise each moment. The unexpected and the unplanned can be blessings when we stay in this creative state of mind. We learn to appreciate surprises rather than be afraid of them. Even when things seem to be in disorder, we can be assured that divine order is present. When we affirm divine order, our eyes open to awesome beauty of creation in everyone and everything. Today, let us understand and appreciate the fact that every unexpected change is part of divine order.

MAY 14 – SPIRIT – I am spirit. Our life experience depends on how we identify. If we identify mostly with the body, we will mostly experience the ups and downs of the material world in a very personal way. From the body's perspective the world is a dangerous place where our largest concerns must be seeking that which we want or think we need and then doing everything possible to avoid the bad outcomes we are sure are coming our way. Ultimately the struggles of the body will all be in vain. Everybody dies, rather, every single body dies, each and every one. So if we are just a body, death is sure. Spirit, however, is eternal. Being spirit, we never really die, we just lay the body aside when it is no longer useful. What happens after that we can't know for sure, but we have faith that something happens. If we identify mostly with spirit, we can have mostly spiritual experiences. We become able to release the cravings of the ego which have previously fueled the suffering caused by identification with the body.

MAY 15 – LOVE – I am love. The love of god within us wants to reach out. The love of god within us is the glue which holds us together; it is spiritual gravity. Let us be not afraid to say "I love you", every time we do it is a celebration of life. As we reach out with love, we allow our words and actions to become the work of our heart. We are blessed by the love of God that moves within and through us. We allow this love to move out from us to bless others. We don't just say it, but we feel this love coming forth in a mighty stream of creation. The sacred presence within us all unites us in a bond of love, now and forever. God's love unites us and sustains us in all of our relationships. Knowing this, we give our very best and in so doing bring out the very best in each other.

MAY 16 – TRUST – I am trusting. I trust God to care for my loved ones. I allow my mind to become one with the mind of God. There is a quality of being, a field of energy that extends from me to those whom I am praying for. I know that when I pray for my loved ones not only are they benefited but so am I and all of those around me. I set up a positive vibration that radiates out in all directions. This is the very love of God, which cares for me, my loved ones and even those who I may not at this time consider loved. I trust this power to see to the wellbeing of family and friends. I do not have to interfere in the lives of others. This presence and power of Creation is working in and through everyone. So I can trust God to care for my loved ones.

MAY 17 – ORDER – I am part of the creation and everything is in divine order. Sometimes it's a mystery, sometimes it's not apparent…when there seems to be some disorder or dysfunction in my life I may wonder what's going on. Later on I will discover that everything was working in and through the divine. Many times divine order is a mystery, and I am grateful for that. Creation is always giving me fresh, new experiences and this can be both exhilarating and a little frightening…but I let go of the fear and rely on divine order to show through the seeming confusion. God is all there is and God is absolute good, so what have I got to be worried about? Divine order is happening right now!

MAY 18 – CARE – I am cared for. I trust God to care for the world. Today, I let go of any burden I may have been carrying concerning the welfare of the world. I may have been worried about war or the economy or just the general state of affairs, but I remind myself that God is everywhere present. The Spirit of creation is moving in and through all life. Sometimes my brothers and sisters have chosen to ignore the presence of God within them and then through the misuse of free will have seemingly caused problems for us all. Again, I remind myself that the presence of the Divine is always offering me and all others only good. All we have to do is to turn our attention to it. Today I know that God is caring for all of creation. So, I let go and trust God to care for the world.

MAY 19 – INSPIRED – I am inspired. I am inspired by the success of others. I am inspired by the success of others, because it lets me know that I can be successful as well. As I notice the people in my life doing well, I am filled with hope for my own wellbeing and the wellbeing of all others. My faith is activated and I perceive the truth, the activity of God is creating goodness through those around me and also through me. This goodness is what is best for me and for all others. I decide to align myself with this good in all that I do. I will work for the common welfare, knowing my own good comes to me most fully when I give good to others. I am inspired to grow and to give in love.

MAY 20 – JUDGEMENT – I am free of prejudice. I am free of fear. Today, I judge rightly. I see myself as a child of Creation. As a child of perfection, I am a perfect creation. As a child of light I am filled with the light of God. Yes…I judge myself perfect, and I judge myself full of light. When I see myself this way, it is easy to also see others as perfect. I understand that God is all. That means God is in all, in me and in everyone else. What a great judgment that is.

MAY 21 – WILLING – I am willing to change. I am willing to change those surface aspects of myself that are sometimes to disturbing. I need to understand that all of my unattractive qualities are just survival tools. These tools are like little cartoon characters that live in my personality. They all think that they are doing the most marvelous job. These character defects, believe that they are helping me cope with the dangers of life. Today, I decide to be free of these characters and free them from their need to "help" me. I let love shine through with no conditions, I release envy with a blessing, I allow myself to be filled with gratitude and all sense of lack melts away. Anxiety dissipates as I move into right action. All anger fades as forgiveness comes to the fore. I am willing, ready and able to heal those fractured characteristics in me. I see them in the light, whole and well, one with God.

MAY 22 – STRONG – I am strong in the light of God. Sometimes I may feel that something is keeping me in place, keeping me from moving on to my greater good. Today, I know that I am strong enough to lift whatever anchor may be holding me in place. I take responsibility for my life and I know that I can soar to new heights by releasing past hurts and regrets. I let go of all guilt and remorse…I forgive all resentments. I can learn from the past, but I can also rise above it. Realizing my oneness with the Divine, I "lighten" up. My mind and heart are cleansed and I move out and up! The very life and light of God are within me, lifting me on high, and I am strong in it.

MAY 23 – FREE – I am free to be. I am free to be and to do whatever is mine to be and do. In the past, I may have been confused and unsure of what my place in the world was. Living and seeing through the filter of past hurts, I have limited myself to reliving all of the old patterns over and over again. No more! I am free, right now. Keeping my attention in the present moment, focusing on the eternal now, I am free. Nothing can harm the real me, because nothing can harm spirit. In the moment, I am clear and I can enjoy life and the people I share life with. My heart's desire speaks to me and through me as I extend love and service to all whom I meet. I claim my inheritance, and I leave the upset and pain of the past behind. Today, I am free to be...I am free to do all that enriches my soul and my life.

MAY 24 – ONE – I am one with God. "The Father and I are one" --John 10:30. – These words attributed to Jesus, are the essence of Jewish tradition, the basis for Christian faith and the very foundation of monotheism. Many would dispute it…some would rather believe that Jesus and God were one but the rest of us are somehow outside of this union. The mediation of John the elder that is the masterwork Gospel of John is so deep and so true and so much on the point. God is One and I am one with God. God is One and you are one with God. In the Christ consciousness there is only oneness. Today I see that the Father and I are one.

MAY 25 – RESPECT – I am respectful. "Truly I tell you just as you did it to one of the least of these who are members of my family, you did it to me" Matthew 25:40 - Very likely words directly from the mouth of Jesus. This is another beautiful reference to our ultimate connectedness. The instruction is to honor and respect everyone, because the presence of God is in all of us. I make a commitment to be kind and caring, to extend love and understanding to everyone I meet today. I honor the presence of God in them and within myself when I give respect to all people. Likewise, I honor the presence of God in all life. I will respect the wild places and the wild things. I will take care to cherish all of creation.

MAY 26 – LIGHT – I am light. "You are the light of the world" Matthew 5:14. Today is a celebration. I see the light of God making Itself evident in my life. I am going to take time to remind myself and others of the good news that we are the light of God the light of the world. I see us all united in joy and thanksgiving. I have been actively developing strong belief in the omnipresence of good in the world and I am filled with an overflowing joy. This happiness flows out as light. No matter how dark things seem to appear, a ray of hope always breaks through and shines before me, showing me the way. The light of God shining through me and others is a beacon guiding my steps. Today I will be focused and ever aware of this light. It is a new day and a new beginning.

MAY 27 – PROSPERITY – I am prosperous. "All things will be given you" Matthew 6:33. Today I notice the gifts of abundance that God gives to me. Visualize a time when someone gave you a particularly wonderful gift. It may have been something you always wanted or it may have been just as beautiful because of the intentions of the giver. Feel the gratitude for the gift and the giver. Now remember a time when you were the giver, feel that generosity. Your heart is full of joy…but this is a small thing compared to the joy of the Spirit that is evident in giving life and form and support to all creation. Remembering the joy of giving you can understand some of the pleasure that God gets from giving us everything we have need of. God gives us the kingdom of prosperity and abundance. God is ready to bless us with that and even more. Today, lets open our minds to receive all that is in store for us.

MAY 28 – PERCEPTION – I am seer. "Do not judge by appearances, but judge with right judgement." John 7:24 Today I use divine vision to see God in every situation. Visualize a rose, see the various distinct shapes and colors of the petals, stem, thorns, and leaves. See yourself as the person painting the rose, capturing the shadowy, indistinct areas around and behind the rose is just as important, because they create a contrast that makes the rose on canvas seem to come alive. All the challenges of life are like this. All the elements of the situation help me perceive the activity of God at work there, including the shadowy areas and the details that may seem unclear right now. Divine vision allows me to judge rightly, not by outer appearances. I rely on the wisdom of God within. I know that blessings are right in front of me, in the light and in the shadows, in what is clear and in what is uncertain.

MAY 29 – TRUST – I am trusting. "The kingdom of God is as if someone would scatter seed on the ground, and would sleep and rise night and day, and the seed would sprout and grow, he does not know how." Mark 4:26-27. Today, I will trust the unfolding universe. There is a divine and mysterious order at work in my life, beyond what I can see or comprehend. I see myself much like a flower, unfolding according to the divine plan. I do not rush the process, or the completion of a project. I listen to Spirit within to know when to act and when to wait. I trust in the mystery of God's process and the divine order that underlies all of life's activities.

MAY 30 – HEALTH – I am healthy. "For life is more than food, and the body more than clothing." –Luke 12:23. I am a healthy and whole creation of God. My thoughts of oneness with God produce actions that are in alignment with creation. These thoughts and actions produce positive results. I nourish myself with ideas of life and healing, I combine these with right eating and time for prayer. I am created whole and well, my soul knows this and resonates health and vitality. My whole body responds to the truth within my soul…I am invigorated. Music, laughter, and words of encouragement uplift me, so whenever I surround myself with family and friends, I receive a blessing. I look around me, noticing the touch of creation. This creation is reflected in me and everywhere I look. I am healthy and whole…a full creation of God.

MAY 31 – TIME – I am giving of my time. All time is our time. We might have tried to divide our time into sections, thinking that a portion is work time, another family time, still another community service time; and of course there is never enough of it. Let's try a different approach, let us decide that all time is our time; our time to spend as we decide. That way all of our time becomes a gift; to ourselves and to anyone else we share it with. In the past we may have sometimes brushed people off with a minimum of concern, we might have even felt that they were pests. Now, don't get defensive; all of us have experienced this at one time or another. Let us realize that by giving time to others we show our concern and respect for them. We know that as we take time to acknowledge and interact with others we are enriched.

JUNE

A hard nut
To crack
Broke open
When you
Appeared.
Now totally
Shattered,
Scattered
At your feet
Waiting to be
Swept up.
Hoping to not
Be discarded
But maybe to be
Baked into your
Sweet cakes.

JUNE 1 – TALENTS – I am sharing my talents. and abilities with the world. As I take stock of my internal assets, I am grateful for the potential that creation planted within me. I have infinite possibilities available to me and these possibilities all generate from the blueprint within my soul. The more I share from these attributes, the stronger they grow. As I give my gifts to the world, my experience and expertise increases…I am also planting new seeds in creation that will bear unexpected fruit in the future. The more I share of myself, the greater my reward and my prosperity. Today, I will freely share my talents and abilities.

JUNE 2 – TREASURE – I am generous with my treasure. There are two kinds of treasure, one is our material wealth. Our money, our property, and our possessions these are treasure. The other treasure is that of our hearts. Those relationships and endeavors that we hold most dear. The principle of generosity can be applied to both. First let us consider material wealth, we may have been taught that when we give some physical thing away we no longer have it. Of course this is true as far as simple arithmetic goes. However, we also know that we live in an abundant universe and that being generous opens us up to receive more. Being generous overcomes the fear of lack, which in turn changes the way we look at the world. In the matter of treasures of the heart, when we give freely of them they grow. So no matter what the treasure our generosity should be the same.

JUNE 3 – ACTIVATION – I am moving from hope to faith. Hope activates my faith. Hope is not a wish, or some poor, tired excuse for a dream. Hope is an energy that opens the door to faith. When we are down, hope lifts us up. From time to time we may feel as everything is falling apart, or that our good is just not coming to us. At such times we can turn our attention to others who have overcome similar or even greater problems. We allow ourselves to be inspired by the victories of others. We can focus on the power of faith that is opening up in us. Faith is our perceiving power and it is brought into sharp relief by hope. Hope leads me the strong belief that we are all connected and that all of our good comes from the same source. Hope activates my faith and restores me to wealth and wholeness.

JUNE 4 – EVIDENCE – I am the evidence of prosperity. Faith is a perceiving power; it applies itself according to what we have faith in. If we have faith in fearful things, we will be afraid. Contra-wise if we perceive abundance we will feel prosperous. This abundance is both within us and all around us. We are in the flow of abundance. We can see ourselves immersed in the wealth and well-being of the universe. This wealth is unlimited; we are unlimited. Paying attention to what we believe, what we think, and what we feel we see that there is a direct connection to what we experience in the world. Our very thoughts go forth to become the evidence of their quality in our lives.

JUNE 5 – REACH – I am reaching out. I reach out to the all-ness of God that surrounds me. Knowing that I am surrounded be the all-ness of God makes it easier for me to stretch and reach out to the good that is mine. This field of Creation is vibrating with spiritual energy and so am I. The energy flows in to me and out from me in a continual cycle of creativity. I am able to perceive what may not be visible, I am able to believe in what may appear to some as inconceivable. I am able to look beyond appearances to the reality that underlies all things. I hear the words of Jesus: "All things can be done for the one who believes." (Mk. 9:23). I reach out to the all-ness to God and I reach right into the magnificence of the universe.

JUNE 6 – FAITH – I am faithful. Faith brings continual blessings into my life. As my reliance on faith becomes more pronounced, blessings continue to flow into my life. Faith is power, it is the perceiving power. It actually determines how we see. We remember the thoughts of Paul: "Faith is the assurance of things hoped for, the conviction of things not seen." With faith, I believe that God is providing for me and in all other ways blessing me—even when there is no evidence that anything is happening. I have faith in God, and that faith fills my soul with joy, every day! I release all worries and concerns. I focus on living right now! My talents and abilities begin to come forth freely—in all my affairs. I recognize that prosperity comes through my faith in God. My faith is furthered when I acknowledge the presence of God. I am grateful for all the gifts that come my way. Faith continues to bring blessings into my life.

JUNE 7 – CONFIDENCE – I am confident in the presence of God. As long as I practice the presence of God, as long as I know that God is always with me, my confidence abounds. I understand that alone I am powerless to accomplish the desires of my heart. Alone, in ego, I have a hard time making a right decision. However, when I begin to work with Spirit to establish and achieve my goals, I am filled with confidence. A renewed energy builds in me and my enthusiasm overflows. I am able to consider a wide range of objectives and I know that with God, I can achieve any of them. The power of creation will work through me to accomplish great and amazing things. With faith in God and confidence in myself, I begin each day anew.

JUNE 8 – RELY – I am trusting. I rely on the creativity that is planted in me. Prosperity is just the result of allowing the creativity in me to come forth. As I allow the divine gifts in me to be expressed in the world, prosperity naturally occurs. This happens without me having to manipulate results, or worry about outcomes. I can trust in God, to work through me, and I know that good will flow through me and to me. Even though the world around me may seem to be changing so fast, I trust the constant presence of God in me. I trust that this presence does not judge me, nor will it ever leave me. I trust that all error, mine and others, can be corrected. I dedicate my endeavors of this day to growing the seeds of greatness in me.

JUNE 9 – LOVE – I am flowing. I move with the flow of the universe. I do not need to resist the ebb and tide of life. I remember the words of Mark 15:39 in their real context. That the life of spirit does not need to struggle and grasp for survival. God is like a life of endless giving, endless loving. To come to the conclusion that Jesus' life was so full that he did not resist hostility, his life was so complete that he had no need to cling to the physical in any way. His capacity to give was without limit, it was total. He held nothing in reserve. As he held nothing in reserve, so also will I give. Again and again the words of Mark echo in me "Truly this man was the son of God."

JUNE 10 – UNBOUND – I am free. From the old Unity song, we hear "I am free, I am unlimited, there are no ties that bind me". Today, let us release all of the old bugaboos that would hold us to fear and uncertainty. As Son of God we are free to do and to be. We are free to cross the boundaries which seem to separate males from females. We are free to accept the outcast. We can enrich our own experience by opening the door to those who are now on the outside. We are free to forgive what we have been told is unforgivable… whatever that may be. We are not bound by the past, our own or anyone else's. We have never been properly served by rejecting those who seemed different…we just continued to affirm a difference that is really not present. We are part of the whole of humanity and the whole of creation itself… we are free from tribe, prejudice, gender, sexual orientation, religion, finitude and fear. We are free…

JUNE 11 – DAWN – I am in the light. God is dawning. God is the light of creation. As this Light dawns on us it signals a new consciousness. We become aware that our lives are not bound by the limitations of the past. We are growing above and beyond traditional ideas of God as the "big guy" in the sky. God is not some unstable, egomaniac who takes pleasure in judgment and retribution. We are moving into a new paradigm. Our vision is clearing as we see that God is not some great person but rather the Power that is. God does not act in our behalf, but acts through us in our endeavors. God is dawning on us, that dawn brings a new reality of God as spirit and as the principle of creation. God is attraction, the glue that holds the universe together, the love that binds us to each and every living thing. God is dawning in breadth and beauty.

JUNE 12 – MATURE -- I am maturing. We are maturing. Today, we put away childish things. We step beyond religion into spirituality. We no longer need the false security of that blanket of ignorance and superstition. We recognize the fears that made us cling to it. The worldwide community is our new family; tribal divisions are a thing of the past. In Christ there is no division at all…neither Jew nor gentile. Buddhist, Taoist, Moslem…none of these describe our new identity. We are evolving into the universal man, the universal woman. This is the process by which we accept our responsibility as Son of God. We are maturing…

JUNE 13 – CALL – I am called. God is calling. We are being called into a new consciousness and expanded state of mind and spirit in which we share creation with God. From Malachi (1:11) "From the rising of the sun to its setting my name is great among the nations, and in every place incense is offered to my name, and a pure offering; for my name is great among the nations, says the Lord of hosts." Here in the Hebrew scripture we here the message of universality. This is the prophet hearing the invitation of God to release his parochial concepts of a limited deity. Wherever the light of the sun goes the name of God, the nature of God goes. In every place Creation is praised and thanks is offered. The world is one world under God, indivisible, with liberty and justice for all? The invitation has arrived, an invitation to the ongoing Kingdom of Heaven unfolding everywhere.

JUNE 14 – FABRIC – I am interwoven. Weave, weave, weave us together…We are all part threads in the fabric of Creation. We are strands woven together in a unity that we sometimes cannot see. Our fear tells that we are separate from the rest of "it", apart from everyone and everything. In the past we may have felt dependent on others, and in this dependence we thought we should become independent. We struggled with a sense of inadequacy on the one hand and superiority on the other. This struggle has kept us from having the true experiences of life. Life cannot be fully lived in the denial that we are an integral part of the tapestry of God. Today, we can see clearly, we can sense the completeness of existence.

JUNE 15 – PRESENT – I am present in God. God is present in me. God is with(in) me. From Psalm 139: 7-12: "Whiter shall I go from thy Spirit? Or whither shall I flee from thy presence? If I ascend to heaven, thou art there! If I make my bed in Sheol, thou art there! If I take wings of the morning and dwell in the uttermost parts of the sea, even there thy hand shall lead me, and thy right hand shall hold me. If I say, "Let only darkness cover me, and the light about me be night," even the darkness is not dark to thee, the night is bright as the day; for darkness is as light with thee." Here it is...a fantastic insight into the truth of the ever-present God. From earliest times, some knew what we now see...God is always with/within us. No matter where we go physically or mentally God is there. This is our ultimate comfort...

JUNE 16 – PART – I am (with)in God. I am part of God…
and I have a part in God. I cannot be apart from Spirit
because I am Spirit. My elder brother Jesus, sends me forth
in Matthew (28:18-20) "All authority in heaven and on earth
has been given to me. Go therefore and make disciples of
all nations, baptizing them in the name of the Father and
of Son and of the Holy Spirit, and teaching them to obey
everything that I have commanded you. And remember, I
am with you in all ways, to the end of the age." Again the
message of universality…follow the law and teach it to all
you meet. The law is that love binds us to God and to each
other. We show that we are with God and in God when we
extend God as we move through our moments and our days.
We carry the good news that all are one, that the Kingdom
of Heaven is One, and that oneness is all there is.

JUNE 17 – EXPRESSION – I am expressing. God loves and lives through us. God is the Ground of All Being. All things grow out of that ground. Not a being, but Being. To touch this ultimate reality, we must learn to love in all circumstances. This is how God expresses through us, no other way but love. Jesus made it clear: "You have heard it said: Love your family and hate your enemy, but I say unto you: Love your enemy and do good to those who persecute you." This is the path to peace. Our expression of God will be as good as our ability to forgive. There is someone in your life that will activate this expression, and it is not the person you feel closest to. It is the one you feel alienated from. See them now, looking for your forgiveness, extending their own to you simultaneously. This is our shared salvation, the only one that is real. In this salvation, God loves and lives through us and as us.

JUNE 18 – BLESSED – I am fortunate. God blesses me. God has blessed us with divine vision. All are blessed with this vision, some of use it more than others. In ancient times those who were believed to use it were called Prophets. It was thought that they had special visits from God. During these visits, God gave instructions and told of the future. It is interesting that, if the future events were negative it was always because the people had sinned, and if the future events were positive it was because God was generous. Some of these folks saw God as the power of love moving in the world, some saw God as the avenging power and some saw God as both. In any event, we can safely assume that the Prophets of old had no powers that we do not. We can see, like they did...but we know that God is not mad at us, so we can go right to the good stuff. This sight is the ability to discern God's Will (goodwill) in our lives. It is the sense that shows us our purpose in life. We are blessed with divine vision...

JUNE 19 – BLESSING – I am a blessing. Gen. 12:3 (to Abraham) "…in you all families of the Earth are blessed", Abram's name was changed to Abraham. God inspired him with the knowledge that he was not just father to his family, but father to multitudes. We can see that he was father to Islam through Ishmael and father to Hebrew and Christian alike through Isaac, his progeny flourished but that is not the great inspiration in the story. We see that Abraham and Sarah live in us wisdom coming together with love to create a multitude of blessings for everyone we come into contact with. We are blessings to all who know us and even those we have never met, each time we extend the love of God through our endeavors.

JUNE 20 – LIGHT – I am a light. We have been advised to be a light to all the nations. Love has called us to carry out goodwill in all that we do. The light of love is in us and goes before us wherever we go. In Isaiah 42:6-7 "I am the Lord, I have called you in righteousness, I have taken your hand and kept you; I have given you as a covenant to the people, a light to the nations, to open the eyes that are blind, to bring out the prisoners from the dungeon, from the prison those who sit in darkness." We hear the great message that we have been called to "righteousness". God, as love, is holding us close. In spirit we are safe to deliver the covenant of love to others. Our task is to gently open the eyes of those who do not see the kingdom, to release those who are held in the prisons, and not just the cells of self-centeredness. We are to dispel the darkness of separation. We are light to all...

JUNE 21 – SERVANT – I am a servant. From Isaiah 49:6 "It is too light a thing that you should be my servant to raise up the tribes of Jacob and to restore the survivors of Israel; I will give you as a light to the nations, that my salvation may reach to the end of the earth." Our service is to light the fire that rouses up all of our kinsmen (everyone), and brings Israel (the nation that strives with God) back to its former relevancy. We are the gift of God (light) to all the nations (universality); that all might be brought into health and wholeness. The creative spirit within us, gives us to the world as a gift for the world's ultimate good. We are the good servants...

JUNE 22 – RESPONSIBLE – I am responsible. We are not victims of the world. We are responsible for our lives and what we bring to those around us. We are not bound by the ignorance or misdeeds of others, even our forbearers. From Ezekiel 18: "he who does not the selfish thing but rather the selfless thing" (paraphrasing) He who does not think of material things in prayer, or love empty things (instead of God), or pursue someone else's husband or wife...who does not wrong anyone...but rather gives what he has to others... this one shall surely live". So no matter what lessons we may have been taught by family or neighbors, friend or enemy, loved one or acquaintance...we know the truth, and the responsibility and the choice is ours. We give love and that is the way we live.

JUNE 23 – LOVE – I am loving. That which we call love, is many times just some needy sentimentality which actually separates us from each other. We sometimes think that the love of another will make us complete. Even if this need is satisfied, we are not filled because it is in the giving not the getting that we are fulfilled. Love is not an emotion. Love is the very life of God. It is the power that binds all creation together. It is the glue that holds the universe together. This love is creation extending itself. We are loving when we extend creation in all that we do. True love is a sense of connection and an extension of goodwill to all. True love happens to us when I feel connected to all life and I desire only good to come to all life. Today, I affirm, I am loving... I am loving...I am truly loving.

JUNE 24 – WISDOM – I am wise. We have the wisdom of God within us. The great seers of the past were our spiritual predecessors. Let us see ourselves and all others through the eyes of wisdom. Today, release all need to judge harshly… from time to time we may have seen ourselves as being "less than", we may have seen ourselves as not measuring up to some standard. We may have even thought ourselves "bad". Viewing ourselves this way, lends itself to also seeing others negatively. Today, let us be the prophets of the new age… today, let us change the way we see. Let us see ourselves as child of God, one with Creation. We, all of us, are integral and irreplaceable parts of the universe. Seeing with the eyes of wisdom is seeing the truth. And the truth is that none can be separated from the goodness of God. This is the good news, in our wisdom let us spread it.

JUNE 25 – RULE – I am guided. (Begin by reading the Book of Ruth in the Hebrew Bible) God is king, in other words God is our leader. Understand that God is the ruling principle of creation. This is the basis of all success and happiness. In Ruth (1:1-5) we learn that a man named Elimelech (Hebrew: God is king) left his home, which was called city of bread (Bethlehem) because of a perceived state of drought. Losing sight of his own namesake, he takes his delightful wife Naomi to Moab. Elimelech thought that he could move away from lack to another place where things would be better. This of course represents the erroneous idea that we can escape from ourselves. Since the operating principle of the universe is cause and effect, if we are experiencing lack in our lives, we have the responsibility and the opportunity to bring prosperity back into our lives. We do not have to run away. We can bloom right where we are planted, once we come back into the idea that God is king in any kingdom.

JUNE 26 – DELIGHT – I am delighted. Naomi, the mother-in-law of Ruth was the epitome of delight until she lost her husband and sons. Then she symbolically changed her name to Mara which means bitter. She blamed God for her loss because she did not understand the principle of cause and effect. Her and her husband had left their land of plenty because of a consciousness of lack. They moved to another country in order to find what was already a part of them. Today let us delight in the ways of Love. We can be happy and content with life as it presents itself right now. In that way we will be prepared to take advantage of the opportunities that creation provides in every given moment. I will remember the "Naomi" parts of me which are named 'sweetness', 'pleasantness', 'beloved', and 'beauty'. These are names that light my heart and lift my spirit so that I am delighted.

JUNE 27 – HEALTH – I am healthy. In the book of Ruth, we read that Elimelech and Naomi have two sons. Those sons were named Mahlon (mild; weakness; disease; sickness; sickly; wasting; pining) and Chilion (in Hebrew means: pining, wasting away, sickly; consumption, destruction). Of course no one really names their children like this. This is a story; it is an allegory that is trying to make a point that when we fall from a prosperous state of mind all of our creations (off-spring) are sickly. Today, let us cast off any misgivings about how we will be cared for. The power of creation has never left us. We have the health of God in us, we cannot be sick. We have the intelligence of creation in us, we cannot lack. We are health and prosperity incarnate, we will thrive.

JUNE 28 – YOUTH – I am youthful. How often have we heard the saying: "You are only as old as you feel."? Well it really is up to us to generate energy and keep ourselves always in high spirits. Orpah in the book of Ruth represents the youth that leaves us. We do not have to suffer this seeming abandonment. Those of us who engage the body in invigorating activity will tend to stay robust. Those of us who keep the mind active, learning and doing new things, will tend to stay alert. Yes, there are still some aspects of us that seem to age, but the more energetic we remain, the more energy we have to spend. Today, let us make a commitment to health and vitality. Let us find some new adventure to participate in. We can learn a new physical skill; we can begin to learn a new language. We can simply start a new book. We are youthful, let's stay that way.

JUNE 29 – LOYALTY – I am loyal. Every character in the Bible represents some characteristic in us. Some of these traits are more apparent than others, some surface from time to time and others are hardly ever noticed. The qualities that Ruth encompasses are some of the more attractive ones. In Hebrew, Ruth means: female friend; sympathetic; companion; desirable; delightful; friendship; pleasing; beautiful…wow, that's a lot. The metaphysical definition of Ruth is: the love of the soul in its natural state, or the love of the natural soul for God and for the things of Spirit. Isn't it interesting that the most obvious trait of Ruth is not even mentioned here, her loyalty? It is that which attracts people to the story. But it is indeed loyalty that grows out of love. So love is the watchword here, and love, we know, is loyal. So as we develop all of these traits within us and we become as Ruth, a lover of truth and loyal to our principles, loyal to our loved ones and loyal to creation.

JUNE 30 – VITALITY – I am strong. In the strength of God, I am confident. I am cheerful, willing, prompt and quick to action. All of these are the assets of Boaz the husband of Ruth. He is a wealthy man, but with great character. He represents the power of thought and the strength of character. When he is wed to love (Ruth) and established in substance (Bethlehem) there is an opening of the way for the birth of the Christ. Through him comes David and finally Jesus. This vitality is an asset in each and every one of us. We have all of these fine attributes in us right now. We can be strong in God because that is our natural state. If we do not feel it, it is only because we are focused on something else, something that is not real. Today, let us revel in our strength. We can be quietly confident in our connection to God and move quickly to right action which will activate the Christ spirit in us.

JULY

Mindless for
A moment;
Lost in self.
Random worry
Spins my mind.
Light playing
Strangely
On the wall
Calls my
Attention
To the vista
Darkening
Out of the window
Blue gray above
Smear of silver
Light between
Black city below
With scattered
Jewels of home-life;
Reveals an alternative
Horizon of hope.

JULY 1 – WORSHIP – I am working with spirit. Here again is the emphasis on service brought forward. Obed is the son of Boaz and Ruth and the grandfather of David. The name in Hebrew means laboring; working; marking; serving; worshiping. It is very interesting that work and worship are connected so intimately in this Obed. The theme is repeated over and over: proper work is the true worship of God and is the result of an awakening of the spirit. The metaphysical meaning is: an active thought, in the spiritual conscience of man, that pertains to service and worship. We remember "God is spirit and they that worship him must worship in spirit and truth (John 4:24). So, knowing that God is divine mind, we think the highest thoughts. We worship by turning our thinking to things that are good and full of Spirit. This shows through in our work and by definition our worship.

JULY 2 – HARMONIOUS – I am harmonious. Nature and Grace are in harmony with me. The physical energy of my body and the spiritual energy of my soul are in harmony. It is only my thoughts of separation that makes this seem not so. My body is part of creation...my spirit is part of creation; they cannot be separate. I may think that my spirit is in disagreement with my body and this creates an invisible but seemingly impenetrable wall, it creates division in me. This wall is coming down today as I decide for harmony. I am working to renew and restore harmony of body, mind and spirit. I invite the wisdom and love of God to shape my thoughts and actions. Harmony works wonders within me, blessing me with peace of mind. Harmony will prevail even in the most difficult times as I acknowledge the presence of God in the midst of me. All of my fragments are united in divine harmony.

JULY 3 – PARTICIPATION – I am a participant in life. I participate in and take joy in life. I do not just sit on the sidelines and watch as time goes by. I am mindful and aware of what goes on around me but I am not just a spectator. I am involved in the ongoing unfoldment of the universe. My involvement starts with taking joy in every part of living. I find golden moments in each day as I connect intimately with Creation. I revel in the creative energy in my body, mind and spirit. I do not deny the physical, I do not denigrate the mental, and I do not ignore the spiritual. I move past any seeming limitations of the past and immerse myself fully in the present. I realize my own sacredness and my sacred link to all life. I realize that I am on holy ground, right now. I experience oneness with God and therefore with everything in my life.

JULY 4 – INDEPENDENCE – I am free. Today is Independence Day! Today, I celebrate my independence from anything which may have caused distress in my life. I declare independence from all negative habits and emotions. I know that there is greater power in me than in the habit, and I surrender to that power. I no longer have to fight to overcome circumstances and events. It is interesting how surrender to the power of God is the very thing that stops the fighting. This power of God within me is the very essence of freedom. It is all the power to do whatever is called for. It is all the power, that I will ever need. Today is Independence Day and I can be free!

JULY 5 – INTERDEPENDENCE – I am interdependent. Let us celebrate the unity of all life. As we walk through the world today, we can take time to notice what is going on around us. We are aware of the connection. We are aware of the interrelatedness. We know we cannot exist apart from each other. It is actually in our one-ones that we have our existence. There is no such thing as a self-made man. Everyone relies on the support of others and the environment, whether they realize it or not. We want to take joy in the realization. We want to give our gifts to others, knowing full well that these gifts are being returned in untold ways. We no longer need to stand alone, on our own; our love brings us fully into life. This then is true freedom, knowing that we are valuable and precious to creation. This principle of one-ness motivates us to become even more involved in life. We allow creation to unfold through us. We find that we have an abundance of energy for whatever interaction that presents itself.

JULY 6 – AMOSIFIED – I am amosified. Read the book of Amos in the Hebrew Bible; it tells the story of simple man of flocks who, in his meditation sees a sorry state of affairs. Historically, it is probably the best of times for the Hebrew people. They are strong in military and in commerce. Prosperity is flowing abundantly to some of the people while others are suffering. This is, of course, nothing new. Some of us will always continue to live outside of abundance for reasons that are not really clear. However, those that are suffering should not be ignored. This was the condition of the time. The poor and needy were the "invisible" people. Amos prophesied correctly that all material things would be of no value if they were the focus of life and that they would eventually dissipate if they were not shared. The King and the Priest in the story represent government and religion, not paying attention to alleviating and healing need. Today let us see if we can do better than most of the characters in this story.

JULY 7 – GOODNESS – I am good. God is all good. Let's take a moment right now to relax into that presence of God, which we know is all good. See yourself going back in time, you are the shepherd, Amos, with your flock grazing on the side of a hill. You are at peace with the world and with your place in it. In the peaceful state you become aware of how all things in nature are working together for good. It occurs to you that all these things working for good are actually in harmony with God, further that they are parts of God. You allow your vision to extend from the hill where you rest, down into the valley and still further into the city beyond. The city is bustling with activity and it is obvious that prosperity abounds. Here and there you notice people who seem to be less fortunate. You see that they are mostly ignored by the majority. This is a shadow and an apparent disharmony. The hand of God touches your heart with compassion. Your mission is to change the scene, first make the needy visible to others and then to work for them to join in creation. Today, let us make it known that the goodness of God is for us all.

JULY 8 – EXTENSION – I am an extension of God. As I go about my life today, I want to be aware that I am constantly using my God-given talents. I am continually creating my experience. I can help create abundance or I can exacerbate lack, for myself and others. God has already provided all of the possibilities for prosperity, all I have to do is focus on selection. Spirit is continually guiding in me in how to extend love out into my world. Spirit fills me with love, light and life…the keys to receiving all prosperity. I am intimately attuned to the activity of all creation… the continuing extension of the kingdom of God. I am an instrument of creation and I bless all those who come into contact with me, this day. I am looking for new ways to extend the kingdom in all that I do…co-creating the richness of life.

JULY 9 – ABUNDANCE – I am abundant. I am alive with the life of God. The life I am experiencing is part of universal life. I feel it moving in and through me. This life is the very energy of creation. I turn my thoughts to that ever-present life of God. That life is the source of all happiness and joy. I am truly prosperous and true prosperity is the absolute supply of everything that I have need of. If I need healing, I trust that the life of God in me is filling my body with healing light. If I need help with a financial situation, I let this life fill my mind with divine ideas which will guide me to an overcoming. The energy of me is my life and the way I extend that energy determines my life experiences. Whatever my want or need, I understand that life is not a constant state of striving but rather it is the medium in which I give and receive, in that order. I am alive with the life of God and that is the original blessing.

JULY 10 – SHARE – I am sharing freely. All other people are part of my family…they are truly brothers in spirit. All living things are part of my family, we are all linked in the life of God. Today, knowing that I cannot be apart from my brothers, I ask the Holy Spirit to guide me in all my interactions with others. This interaction is more than kind words; it is an ongoing work of service. I am aware that I cannot truly prosper at the expense of anyone else. My abundance and theirs is truly one. As I give to others, I receive in abundance. I love all of God's creations, seeing that we are all one family. I bless and encourage all forms of life that come into my life. Divine love shines in me and from me, giving radiance to the world. I am one with all life.

JULY 11 – SIGHT – I am seeing clearly. I have the gift of divine vision. I use my divine vision to co-create with God. I am able to use my thoughts to create a new reality. I have a vision of prosperity for everyone. I see an abundance of good for the entire world. I know that I can help this vision become reality. As I sit quietly, I feel my heart fill with love. When it is filled to overflow, I extend this stream of love out into the world. I see my family and friends receiving this love as a continuous stream of light. I am just the facilitator, I trust God to give them their own vision and show them how to express their own gifts. I expand my vision to see this light moving over my community, blessing and awakening all of those whom it touches. My vision grows still larger as the light extends across the country, healing divisions as it does. The light encircles the planet bringing peace and harmony to the whole world.

JULY 12 – PRINCIPLE – I am principled. There is nothing that can separate me from the Good that God has for me. I am the herald of the coming of the Lord. This is not some superstition. God is trying to act through each of us every day. Today I will pay attention to this guidance. I bring my attention to the Truth, focusing on principles. I am not on this path by chance. I have divine appointments to keep. My personality cannot keep me from my mission and the personalities of others cannot distract me from my purpose. I will keep my thoughts centered on God; and God will keep me centered in principle. I will continue on my journey giving and receiving blessings as I go. My life is a pillar built on the rock of principle and I see that my life joined with the lives of others is helping to support many good things.

JULY 13 – HARMONIOUS – I am in harmony with others. I bring body and mind into harmony which in turn brings harmony into all relationships. I give myself over to the presence of God in me and in doing so I realize oneness with creation. I am goodwill in action as I perceive myself and all others in Light. I open myself to Life and to divine order. I release all disease in my mind and body. The strength of God flows through me allowing forgiveness. I am focused in and centered on this moment. My vision is single and I am full of energy to complete all of tasks this day. I am in harmony with God, and therefore I am in harmony with all others.

JULY 14 – EXTENSION – I am an extension. We extend the light of love to everyone. We visualize the light in the heart moving through the body and then extending out from us to touch everyone. We are extended by Creation and we extend ourselves in a like manner. We give to the universe and the universe gives to us. We understand that everything we do is an extension of Creation. We are deeply involved in the unfolding good of the universe. Our presence is the harbinger of good things for everyone around me. We stay fully conscious of our ability to enfold the person in front of us, as well as any room that we may enter or the building where we work, or even the entire world.

JULY 15 – CONNECTION – I am connected to those who came before. Today as I remember my forbearers I am filled with courage and energy. I have genetic ancestors, a line of life that extends back into the mists of time, these are my predecessors, those who prepared the way for me. I can honor them in my memory and in my moment to moment living. Their spirits are eternal, just like mine, so they are really still available to me. I also have other forbearers, mentors, historical figures who have inspired me, and anyone else who helped me develop into who I am today. I honor them also. I realize that we are all part of the great web of life that is not limited in time and space. I honor all of those who came before, when I remember them and then act in a manner that reflects favorably on their teachings. I am connected to those who came before.

JULY 16 – BRIDGE – I am the bridge for those yet to come. Just as I am still one with those who proceeded me, I span the present to the future for those yet to come. I am conscious of the fact that I am role model to the young. I am aware that the acts of today impact tomorrow. I pay attention to my words and actions so that they can be a positive example. Just as my ancestors and those who inspired me were a bridge from their time to mine, I am likewise for those who come after. This is both honor and responsibility. To help keep the planet intact, to contribute to the growing store of knowledge, to stand for freedom and equality, to extend love and teach harmony…all of these are a rich inheritance. I intend to will all of these things to the future, for I am the bridge for those yet to come.

JULY 17 – BLESSINGS – I am happy for the good fortune of others. Any time that I may be jealous of another's good fortune, I stop and change my mind. I understand that by begrudging the good of others, I block my own. Today, I celebrate the good that comes to us all. I bless others and I become a blessing to others. If I see success happening for someone, I emulate them. I look for ways that I can learn from their example. Today, I turn envy into blessings, I know that when I acknowledge that my brother deserves the good that comes to him that I am also opening the way for my own good to come to me. So, I am happy…I celebrate the good fortune of others.

JULY 18 – PRAISE – I am praising. Today, we look for things to praise. Let's be focused on finding the good. We can constantly find new things to praise. We see much that is worthy in our families, friends and co-workers and we take the time to tell them so. We notice the wonder in life, and we speak of it. Every time we find something to praise, the power of love grows in us. We should also learn how to better accept praise. When someone compliments us, it is unseemly to mumble some falsely humble denial. Practice acceptance with a simple "thank you". To think that we are not worthy of praise is arrogant and also puts everyone else in the same leaky boat. Today see that praise is a continuous flow…we give it out and it comes back.

JULY 19 – WONDER – I am awed by the wonder of creation. I cannot wait to get out into the world today. I am excited about the prospects of this new day. Today, I will participate in life, I will not sit as a spectator on the sidelines. I will notice with appreciation all of the beauty around me and then I will interact appropriately with it. I am inspired and I want to give back to the wonder that spawned the universe. So today, I understand that I give to life in direct proportion to the inspiration that I draw from it. If I pay close enough attention to the beauty that is all around me, I will be able to give ever so much more.

JULY 20 – PASSION – I am filled with a passion for living. I am aware that passion can also mean suffering. But today, I mean something else entirely. I give my attention to the call to life that stirs in my being. Physically, my body is alive with the passion of the flesh. Mentally my mind is alert with a passion for new wisdom. Spiritually my being is awakened with a passion for creation. I will no longer try to stifle it, because this passion that I feel is natural and good. It needs to be shared and I can share appropriately and in a creative way. I have no need to control others, I release them to pursue their own passion.

JULY 21 – STAND – I am standing for something. Today, we stand for good. We give our time and energy to the accomplishment of positive goals. We do not resist seeming evil but rather we look for ways to bring more good to the situation. We stick to our convictions and remain true to our values. When we see injustice and suffering, we need not participate in some moral outrage. It is very unlikely that fighting will have any good and lasting effect, regardless of the great temptation and temporary justification we may feel. Examining the events, we begin with awareness and then move to acceptance. It is what it is but whatever it is, it can be changed or the aftermath can be healed. This is our task, to act with compassion to alleviate suffering.

JULY 22 – LOVE – I am compassionate and full of gratitude. I pay attention to those around me. I listen with open ears, an open mind and an open heart. I establish empathy and that leads to compassion which turns to unconditional Love. I show this love by being truly helpful. Through kind actions, I show the value of life. Life is good just as it is, and I am grateful for it. I celebrate what is. I am not afraid to live life as it is. I do not fantasize about what "should" be nor do I commiserate with others in the same vein, but rather I accept the way things are now with a grateful heart and then do the necessary work to bring about any desired change.

JULY 23 – POWERFUL – I am powerful? We know that our words are powerful. Today, we remember that when we speak the word of power, it is so. Today, we can tell the truth. The truth as we know it. We will not cover up, or sanitize or minimize or distort it. We will tell it or we won't say anything at all. We will pay attention to the thoughts that lead to our words and we will keep them positive. Positive words can be gifts to others. It is important that we compliment rather than criticize. Just as we are careful about the words that come out of us, we should also be aware of those we take in. We do not need an excess of anything to feel better. We are filled with the spirit of creation, the creative, positive things we say will manifest in our lives.

JULY 24 – CREATIVITY – I am totally involved in creation. I realize who and what I am. I am son of God, inheritor of the Kingdom. I am co-creator of my life and circumstances. I understand that everything that has happened in my life up until now and everything that is going to happen has been and will be a direct result of all of my creative activity (or non-activity). I know that cause and effect is the mechanism of creation. I am equal in creative power to everyone else and everyone else is equal to me. I do not denigrate myself or others. In total humility I know that I am part of Creation and so is everyone else.

JULY 25 – EXTENSION – I am an extension. When God created us he merely extended himself. He is still extending himself now. We, who are made of him, are also extending. When we are awake, we create as God created; sending love forth into all situations and that love forgives and changes seeming evil into good. We also misuse our ability by projecting. When we are spiritually asleep we think that we can change God's work...we think that perfection is not...we think that we have an evil nature...we think that we make ourselves what we are. These are all insane beliefs. Today, let us unravel these nightmarish thoughts, let us untie the knots in our thinking. Let us know the truth that God created all and that all that God created is Good.

JULY 26 – INVULNERABLE – I am invulnerable. Today is the day that we release doubt and fear. We will establish the "peace of God which passes all understanding". Let use our power of elimination to release any thoughts that we can be harmed. Throughout the day, whenever an anxiety, nervousness or fear shows itself let it go. Do not attempt to suppress these feelings, just acknowledge that the fear is an error and then gently release it. Now allow a sense of calm to descend upon you...establish a peaceful place in your mind...and then extend that peace out from you to your body and then to everything else that you can see close to you. Mentally extend this peace to every person in sight. Tell yourself that just as you are invulnerable so is everyone else.

JULY 27 – ALTAR – I am the altar. Commitment to the Source is our task today. We can be totally invested in Creation because there is nothing else that is worthy of investment. Becoming one with the One is a total commitment. There is nothing to lose, everything of value is already ours. Protecting the body or the body's possessions is a preoccupation of the ego but when we care for spirit the body is automatically cared for. The "body is the temple of the lord" is just the beginning of understanding of the true temple. The true temple is not built of stone or of flesh. Its beauty can only be seen with spiritual eyes because it is the very spirit of us. The altar is the part of me upon which I lay the offering of forgiveness. It is the place where we recognize that Creation and its creations are all totally dependent on each other.

JULY 28 – HEAL – I am healing. We are not sick. The body cannot be sick without the mind's cooperation. In our present world, the body is. Do not deny or abuse the body, rather realize that it also invulnerable when served by proper mind-action. If you believe in medicine, take the medicine…but take it with the realization that it is your mind that will activate the healing. Physical healing is the province of the mind; mental healing is the province of the spirit. All will be accomplished perfectly when all of our errors have been forgiven. All of our errors will be forgiven when we truly see that these are not indelible sins, but mistakes that can be corrected. Forgiveness and healing are one, just as my brother and I are one.

JULY 29 – FEARLESS – I am fearless. We are afraid only to the extent that we cannot release the material world. The more willing we become to let go of everything we think we need the less fear we will have. Letting go does not mean giving away all of our possessions it just means being willing to. We can step out of the nightmare of self-centeredness, we can release our obsession with needing more, we can eliminate our compulsion to gather more stuff. Without attachment we are without fear. Without fear we are without anger. Without anger we are at peace

JULY 30 – MIRACLE – I am miracle minded. Be ready for a miracle today. A miracle is the realignment of perception…it is forgiving the appearance of evil…it is forgiving a sense of lack or a feeling of danger. Being miracle minded means that we are prepared to accept a miracle in place of a problem. As the day unfolds, take every opportunity to change fear into love. Miracles blossom from the seeds of love. Miracles are not magic…they are just the right application of principle. Spirit is already perfect…you are spirit…your brothers and sisters are spirit…see that and miracles will occur continuously.

JULY 31 – HARMONY – I am in harmony. Harmony is the acceptance of one-ness. When we hear the phrase "All things work together for good, for those who love God." What do we think? Do we imagine it means that if we worship "hard" enough or long enough that God will intercede and change our experience? Do we think perhaps that it means that those few who God loves will experience good? Well, it means neither of these...it means that when we love the All-ness of God, then All things come together as one. This is the establishment of harmony, but it really does not change reality which is already in harmony it just allows us to experience it. When we extend love to all, all reflects that love back to us.

AUGUST

Perception
Does not see,
It constructs.
From a design
To avoid pain
And find pleasure
Perception builds
A world apart
From reality.

AUGUST 1 – CHARITY – I am charitable. Charity is healing. True healing is accomplished through the application of proper charity. When we see the perfection in another, we are practicing proper charity. Today, let us realize that when we notice something less than perfection in someone else we are straying from the mark. If a person seems troublesome it is because they need help...it is our place to give assistance. We can offer our clear vision and know that the other can also see it. This single act of charity will move us all closer to the truth of our Being.

AUGUST 2 – TIMELESS – I am timeless. We actually exist outside of time. Our spirits are not impacted in any way by time or space. It is just our present experience that seems to be in a linear order, in a certain place. As we practice forgiveness of and for our brothers we are moving from this place and time toward the eternal kingdom. Our love heals by correcting the misperceptions brought about by egocentricities. The ego sees everything in terms of judgement and projection. It is continually trying to get the thing(s) that it thinks will make everything better... this never works. The ego is insane, but we are not. The ego presents guilt and shame for each mistake perceived...spirit sees innocence and an opportunity to heal. Spirit keeps us in the present moment, which is really eternal...timeless.

AUGUST 3 – CORRECTION – I am correcting. In order to correct mistakes (forgive) I must release all judgment of the person or situation. Forgiveness is not absolution; it is not extending magnanimously to one less fortunate. It is not giving something to someone that they don't already have. Correction is not saying "Oh, yes...you have hurt me but I am going to let it go." This approach is the way of ego superiority. The forgiveness that corrects is the ability to totally let go of the event or perceived injury. Let our forgiveness be a healing balm of forgetfulness. Neither seeing nor holding a grievance...neither comparing or contrasting...but rather embracing our brother in the light which comes from within. This is correction...this is forgiveness.

AUGUST 4 – MIND – I am of one mind. One-mindedness is our true state. It is when we become single (minded) that we are practicing the First Commandment most purely. There is naught save God; we share the mind of God. We co-habit the Kingdom with God. True oneness is the ultimate reality that we seek to return to. In time and space, we are always somewhat removed from this state. As time unravels we continue to see the present through the filter of the past. If we use time as a learning device, we will begin to truly live with each other and for each other. We practice single mindedness, reminding ourselves of the ultimate state which we yearn to return to.

AUGUST 5 – AVOCATION – I am practicing. Our job is much more than the work of our hands, heads or even our hearts. Our job is more than our vocation…our true work is creation of the highest order. This high order creation is simply the extension of our true selves into all that we do. Our true self expresses as the love of God moving through all of our affairs. Avocation is the practice of art and talent and effort all focused on the goal of loving reconciliation. Our avocation shows itself in our loving treatment of others and our pursuit of goodwill in regards to others.

AUGUST 6 – HELP – I am helpful. Our job is to be of service. We are son of our father and as son we are to be active in the father's business. We are representatives (in the image) of our father. God has extended us into existence and we exist to extend further. All throughout this day I will look for opportunities to give that which is most important. I will give proper service, doing the right thing, for the right reason, at exactly the right time. I will be helpful and that help will give love to all whom I meet.

AUGUST 7 – DIRECTION – I am directed. As we move through the experiences of these moments we can release anxiety and nervousness. There is nothing which will occur that we have not already been provided with. Relaxing into the presence of spirit we will be guided as to our speech and our action. We are in exactly the right place and in this place we are never alone. Our impulse to help comes from the gentle urging of spirit within. As we follow this direction, doing that which we are prompted to do our direction is clear and we are not conflicted. Restoration is the order of the day and as we help to restore others we learn to be restored.

AUGUST 8 – JUSTICE – I am just. I support divine justice. Divine justice is cause and effect in action. I understand that when I set events in motion there will be costs and consequences. The results could be called karma or they could be called rewards and punishments. I know that if I begin with concern for the common welfare and a sense of responsibility for those around me, my actions will generally bring good to all. If I do not have this focus, the consequences will become apparent. I will be on the outside looking in and I will cause harm to myself and others. Because divine justice is always present, the opportunity for good will be present even in the midst of a calamity. Each of us has the ability to choose the good no matter what our behavior or someone else's behavior has been.

AUGUST 9 – CONSCIOUSNESS – I am consciousness. We are part of universal consciousness. We share the Divine mind. Self-consciousness is not a part of this shared mind; it is the thought system of the ego. The ego is wrong-minded and interprets incorrectly. Today, let us release all self-consciousness. Willingness to let go of self-centeredness is the beginning of peace. Actually letting go is bliss. All of this involves practice. Our practice is the conscious decision to be non-judgmental at every opportunity to judge…to be uninhibited when we would rather be self-conscious… to give love when we are about to be overcome with fear. Perception changes as we practice…practice unites the knots in our thinking. Self-conscious no more, we know consciousness.

AUGUST 10 – RELEASE – I am released. Let us pay attention to what we ask for. All of our preferences, perceived needs, wishes, and longings are requests. God has already given us everything. When we ask for anything other than the ability to see our true state of affairs, we confirm lack. The ego wants, the ego needs. Spirit knows that "to have" and "to be" are the same, ego does not. We already have everything because we are everything. This sense of inclusiveness, of belonging is the release from bondage to continual seeking. Say to yourself "I am released...I am released from bondage." Feel yourself entering into God's Kingdom...this is the realm of the One...it is the home of One-ness. You are calm and at peace...this is your sane mind.

AUGUST 11 – HEAR – I am listening. Today, let us listen to the Voice for God. Spirit is always present. Throughout the day, whenever we are judging someone as let us change our mind by listening to Spirit. Whenever we are unhappy, spirit is saying "this need not be". Let us choose joy. We can teach ourselves to think with Spirit…we can think what Spirit thinks and we can stop thinking what Spirit would not think. We can learn to do what Spirit would do and we can learn to not do what spirit would not do. Our minds are one with God's mind, looking at it as if we are separate has literally split our mind and cause interminable suffering. Through listening to the Voice for God we can reunite with that one mind and end our pain. If we are sad, spirit says, "Know that this need not be" …. depression comes from a sense of being deprived of something we think we need… decide instead for abundance. When we are anxious Spirit is there, saying "Know that this need not be" …. anxiety is the mischief of ego. When we feel guilty we just need remember that although ego tries to violate the laws of God, we do not…we cannot. Listen to the Voice for God…at every discomfort it is saying "This need not be".

AUGUST 12 – OVERCOMING – I am overcoming. Be aware of the temptations of personality. The ego is always offering that which has no value. It is dis-spiriting to engage with it. Today, let us focus on overcoming un-truth. We can soar above listlessness. We can be healed of our mistaken ailments. If we engage with God, putting our attention on the things of spirit we be tired no more. Every day we have many opportunities for joy, every day we have been cheating ourselves out of them. We have unlimited power for good. We limit ourselves by judging falsely. Visualize yourself joining with the One and then shining the light of love on all the dark places. The ego is literally shined away in this endeavor. Feel it right now…you have joined yourself with the Father and all is well. This is the true overcoming… shine your light (which is the light of God) on every seeming problem. Notice that as this light shines it draws all living things to it…everything is made One thing. Feel the healing power of love as it reintegrates us all into the kingdom.

AUGUST 13 – DEFENSELESS – I am defenseless. We have no need to defend. At the essence of spirit, we cannot be threatened, there is nothing that would or could harm us. In the Kingdom of God there is no danger. In unity we are protected and cared for. It is only when we consider the wrong-minded idea that we are alone that fear can enter. At every turn when you are tempted to judge a brother as a threat, stop for a moment. Reconnect and be one with him...doing so makes you One with Him. Let us settle for nothing less than this...for this is sanity. So anytime today when the fear comes say to yourself, "I am one with God, of what should I be afraid?" If some person should seem to be causing us grief then say to yourself "I am one with my brother, and this one here is my brother." We can be defenseless because we cannot lose, we cannot be cheated, we cannot be hurt, we cannot be abandoned.

AUGUST 14 – MIRROR – I am a reflection of Good. Ask yourself what do I want to represent…light or dark? Sometimes we may see ourselves darkly in the mirror of the ego, but we need remember that this is a distortion. Get quiet and say to yourself: "I will not look at the egos dark imaginings". Say: "I know that these images are false." Then realize that Spirit is shining on you and that you are a mirror of truth. Goodness shone on us at our inception and brought our mind into being. Goodness shines on us right now and must shine through us. Ego is powerless and cannot prevent the light from coming to us, but we can allow the ego to impede the light that shines through us. Decide now for the light, reflect not darkly. Decide now and continue to decide to reflect the Good.

AUGUST 15 – VIGILANCE – I am vigilant. Today, let us be vigilant for truth. The ego stands guard, ever vigilant to keep truth at bay. The primary motivation of the ego is to maintain a sense of loneliness. This, of course, it hides. Instead it presents control over the immediate environment as the overriding importance. Control is an alternate to sanity. Sanity says that everything is already in divine order and all is well. The need to control speaks to the underlying feeling that we are unsafe, this keeps us unbalanced and paranoid. Paranoia is not the kind of vigilance we really want. Pre-occupation with problems is just one more symptom of insanity…these problems which we sometimes think come with life are actually designed to be insolvable in any meaningful way…one just follows another. Be vigilant for truth…thoughts of inclusion and unity, thoughts of love and service, these are reflections of God the Good Omnipotent…think on these things and be vigilant to maintain them. Here is sanus… our health and wholeness, here is salvus…our safety.

AUGUST 17 – TEACHER – I am teaching. I am willing to teach and to learn. To truly use this tremendous power of example for the good of all we must become involved in change. We must become active in rebuilding the political landscape. We must start to work with a new economic model, one based on what's best of the great System of life in which we are all a part. To weave a new social fabric with the common welfare in mind, to reinvent the nature of education, these are the building blocks of the life we seek. We seek this not just for ourselves but for the good of all. Let us teach immersion in the river of life. We can teach people to flow in the direction of their talents and abilities, and not to fight the currents of uniqueness. In this river the gifts of the individuals come together to join with the greater gifts of oneness and every living thing benefits. Teach will to learn will; practice willing your life and you live the life you will. This is the ultimate vision of the book of Amos. Coming back into alignment with creation and the entire house of David is regenerated.

AUGUST 18 – GIVE – I am giving. Today we practice release. As we learn to release all material things we become free from lack. Only willingness is required...we do not actually have to give away everything, we just have to be willing to do so. This means that if we are called to give, we are able to give without fear. As we give our sense of loss dissipates. Spirit is leading us into the kingdom of heaven. The physical is not of the kingdom. The kingdom is spirit. Being and having are the same...having depends on giving. Let us give completely and without attachment...this will lead us to the door of oneness...the very gates of heaven.

AUGUST 19 – PEACE – I am at peace. Tell yourself: God is. God is one. God is one with me. God is one with all living things. God is one and I am at peace. I will continue to remind myself that no matter what occurs in the outer world, no matter what appears to be threatening, I am one with God and all is well. In this way I will learn peace so that I can teach peace...by continually remembering this oneness, I have peace by teaching peace so that I learn peace. I remember that I must teach what I must learn.

AUGUST 20 – VIGILANT – I am vigilant. I believe in the unity of all life…all living things are connected and truly one with all other living things. This is the ultimate truth of Being. The God of Love is the One God. Vigilance then is required not to establish this truth, which is really unassailable, but rather to filter out any thoughts which are in conflict with this universal principle. So today, I will pay attention to my thoughts and I will ask Spirit to purify any of them that are of conflict and separation. I will remain vigilant and I will gently release any contradictory thinking into the care of Spirit.

AUGUST 21 – HARVEST – I am blessed by the harvest. I have reaped what I have sown…I continue to harvest that which I am planting. This harvest is a great blessing. My thoughts are like seeds that I plant into the fertile ground of my mind. These seeds grow into a crop which manifests itself in my experience. If I plant weeds, I will get an undesirable crop…If I plant good nutritious things, I will be sustained by the what is produced. Spirit is always available to help me choose that which is good and right so that I can sow the best seed and then reap the finest fruit…a blessing indeed.

AUGUST 22 – INCREASE – I am increased. Ideas…Ideals of good are increased in the sharing. Darkness being illusory cannot be shared, but it is projected by the split mind onto other fragments. Dark thoughts of anger or fear should not be denied, we just notice and accept that we are having them then release them to Spirit. Our inner guide will untie the knots in our thinking…cleansing all thoughts of harm and attack. God will never act against us, but he will take darkness from us if we ask because it does not belong in our Mind. Ideas of love and life take the place of revenge and we are all increased.

AUGUST 23 – SINLESS – I am sinless. When the bible says: "I will visit the sins of the fathers unto the third and fourth generation" what do we think? Do we believe that God punishes our children for our mistakes, or perhaps that we are being punished for our ancestor's errors? The sins of the fathers are impacting lives only because cause and effect is in operation. We can be freed from these ghosts of the past simply by forgiving them and allowing spirit to heal the situation right now. This will actually change the past (for us). Past mistakes can be undone by our present forgiveness.

AUGUST 24 – LIVE – I am life. We are eternal life and we will not perish (die). The scriptural words: "the wicked shall perish" is not a portent of some future retribution on bad people. It is actually a description of the Atonement. What it is saying is that our seeming wickedness will be undone. Being undone is the same thing as saying untied or even unbound. The thought system of fear is a veritable knot of lies that bind us to a life of misery. This wonderful statement is a promise that we will be freed from our bondage... we will be off the karmic wheel and we will escape the continual cycle of life and death. We are life and when our misperceptions are undone we will actually know that we are part of that eternal life.

AUGUST 25 – GIFT – I am gifted. God gives the best to me. Although sometimes I don't see it, Spirit is always offering miracles. My perception of the world notwithstanding, only the Love of God is real. Grace blesses me at all times and in all places. Today, I look for signs of goodwill. I will accept my wellbeing with faith in its ultimate benefit. I know that I will receive whatever it is that I request. I just need to request what I really want. Releasing guilt, I am worthy of happiness. Releasing judgment, I am aligned with wisdom. Releasing fear, I am filled with love. I remember that I am never alone…I see the gift of God everywhere.

AUGUST 26 – GRATITUDE – I am grateful. I give the best to God. I am so grateful for my gifts. Today, I will give my best to God, I will give my best to everyone I meet and in all situations in which I find myself. I will release all thought of sacrifice or lack. I know that when I give freely, more gifts freely flow to me. It is a joy to give my best, my best at home, my best in the workplace, my best in the community. The good that is in me wants to express through me and today I will allow it. I am free of all suffering whenever I am intent on being and giving my best.

AUGUST 27 – FEARLESS – I am fearless. We forgive all fear. We are the holy son of God. Spirit smiles on us with love and tenderness, deep and dear. The universe smiles back to Itself remembering it shares holiness with us. All of the love of God is bestowed upon us. Brotherhood and Fatherhood are one and complete. Together, we are without sin and perfect in the eyes of God. Therefore, let us forgive all fear, for if God sees it not, how can it be real. In whole sinless-ness we remember Miester Ekert's words "We are all Words of God, books about God."

AUGUST 28 – MERCY – I am safe. God asks no sacrifice. We are not asked to any sacrifice to find mercy. No sacrifice is needed for peace. The mercy and peace of God are free. To believe that God expects something of us is to forget that He is already the all of us. He does not have to expect, He knows. He knows us as Son, he extends all goodness to us as a result. The only cost to Salvation is that it be freely given and received, by definition then it cannot be purchased. God asks no sacrifice.

AUGUST 29 – LAW – I am love. We give love to all and it becomes a gift to our self. The law of giving and receiving is ancient and true. Whatever we give will be our own reward. Sometimes we lose track of true value. We may believe that by giving, we are reduced by that amount. Today, let us turn those false thoughts aside. Let us stop withholding the good and let us stop giving the negative. Our gift to our brother is indeed our gift to ourselves. If we make a present of peace and extend it out, it returns to us. Extend a blessing and be blessed. To have love, give love. To have time, give time. To have treasures, give treasures.

AUGUST 30 – FORTUNE – I am fortunate. I extend good fortune. The goodness of the universe is extending to us at all times. The good in our lives is a reflection of miracles. We are son and heir to God. The law of love is universal and today we continue to practice it. Even in the midst of seeming chaos and conflict the law of giving and receiving is apparent. If we give from our fear, it increases. If we give from peace we become a center of peace. When we extend the good fortune that comes to us we receive even more.

AUGUST 31 – ENVELOPED – I am enfolded. The peace of God envelops me. Today, let's awaken to the truth. There is nothing but God. We are always in the midst of the divine. To realize this is to find the peace that passes all understanding. Think about how simple this idea is…we are always and forever one with the Source. We are enveloped in the light of God love. We rest in this love, we relax into this presence and we remember nothing but the peace of God. As awareness of this peace grows in us, we become a center of peace for others. We come to understand that our own wellbeing depends on us giving peace to those around us. It is so natural and happens with such ease that it is not a burden. The peace of God envelops us and it is a joy to spread it.

SEPTEMBER

This destruction
Takes too long
Small self
Rock hard
Against the
Love flow
This
Smallness,
A jagged
Wedge
Attempting
To split
A river
Of Light
All to no avail
Time, illusion
Notwithstanding,
Wears me down
Smooths my edges
Eventually turns
Me into We

SEPTEMBER 1 – TEACH – I am taught. Spirit is informing me right now. If we are quiet we will hear the voice for God which resonates deep within. Spirit knows that which we have need of and is trying to teach us at all times and in all places. Release the false and embrace the truth. We are the perfect son of God. Whereas our mind has been split, we can now see oneness. Spirit is the link to the mind of God which has been blocked by our fear. Release any anxiety and relax into the protection of Love. Creation is continually sending joy. Release sadness and take on the joy of God. Spirit is teaching, I am taught.

SEPTEMBER 2 – WAKE – I am awakened. There is a gentle voice calling us to consciousness. We have been sleeping, and dreaming. We have been dreaming a fearful dream of loneliness. The voice of Spirit is calling us out of this nightmare. It is reminding us that the long night is over and the dawn is come. We are assured that we are safe right now. Spirit is awakening us and teaching us the difference between sleeping and waking. Asleep we fear the dark; awake we revel in the light. Recognizing the dream, we are no longer subject to it. Let us remember the light so that when darkness seems to come we can recall the dawn. We are awakened.

SEPTEMBER 3 – WISE – I am wise. Spirit imparts simple wisdom. It does not teach through fear; it does not even remind us of the fear. Spirit does not avoid, but rather approaches with love. We are instructed to do likewise. Everyone who comes to us is both our student and our teacher. We have a gift for them and they have one for us. Spirit does not admonish us, so we do not correct others. We are not taught through fear, so we should not teach through fear. We instruct only positively, saying: "Do only that which is helpful". We teach and we learn by imparting the sense "See good only". We are wise and teach wisdom when we forgive any appearance of lack. We are wise and we are teaching wisdom.

SEPTEMBER 4 – INNOCENT – I am innocent. Spirit is not keeping track of our errors. It sees through the error and forgives any seeming problem. Anytime we feel less than or that we have sinned, or made mistakes…we can ask Spirit to show us the truth and we can correct the error through forgiveness. The light always answers…it shines through fear with the love of God. All of the mistakes of the past are washed away in a torrent of light…neither staining nor punishing…correction is made by choice. Today, let us choose innocence.

SEPTEMBER 5 – GENEROUS – I am generous. Spirit is generous. We are able to give all in order to have all. We cannot give that which we do not have…therefore, we can give all because we have all…there is no lack. We already have all because we are all. This is not a material thing, although it can show itself in material things, true giving is the extension of the love that comes to us from creation… extending it out to all creation. We cannot lose by giving, we can only gain more. As has been stated, this is not material giving, but it can translate into material giving if we are so guided. To be generous just means that we give our all. This can seem like work but actually it is a light burden. Whatever is called for that is what we give. Spirit will tell us what and when, we just need to be willing and ready.

SEPTEMBER 6 – CALM – I am calm. Spirit is peaceful. Today, let us just relax. Before we engage in any task we must first relax. It is suggested that we begin each day with prayer and meditation…this sets the tone for what is to come. If we should forget, it is not a problem, we just stop and get quiet when we remember…just take a moment to become centered. Anytime we find ourselves nervous or anxious, we can pause and re-center. When we are calm and at peace, we feel a sense of wellbeing and we also are able to give peace to our surroundings. Many are the times that we can act as an agent of positive change when we are able to come to peace. Our presence becomes a blessing to all those around us and an example to all those who are watching. I am calm, I am at home, I am at peace. This is a tremendous boon to my brothers and a lesson for myself.

SEPTEMBER 7 – ATTENTION – I am attentive. The first gift is the gift of attention. As my brothers come before me today, I will give them my kind attention. I will allow Spirit to show me who they truly are. I will listen to their words, allowing Spirit to translate. I will look only for the good, and I will be uplifted by what I observe. As I am buoyed, so will I raise the one with whom I interact. I am paying attention… looking for the presence of God in all that I observe. Spirit is helping so that I am able to release any fearful appearance and concentrate on the truth. If I am attentive, I can see the light of God in everyone and everything…and then I can respond by returning that light.

SEPTEMBER 8 – LIMITLESS – I am limitless. We are endowed with limitless power to create our lives. God created us in his image and that requires us to create as God creates. We extend of ourselves and that extension orders our lives. It is important to understand that God is our creator… we are not God's creator. We do, however, maintain the characteristics of our holy parent. We are holy and our power to create is limitless. Our powers are much deeper than we generally appreciate. Over time and with practice we will see more clearly. Right now we can at least observe that our choices are the cause of how our lives proceed. We are not the victim of the world, but rather we have created our experience (world). Once we have accepted this fact we can move forward and begin to consciously design our lives. We are limitless and as we extend ourselves it becomes apparent that we can extend ourselves ever further.

SEPTEMBER 9 – OBSERVE – I am observant. Observing the presence of God in all things is the path to peace. God is continually offering us only good. Anything else that appears is the result of the misinterpretation of the ego. The ego wants equal rights with God, the ego wants our attention so it tries to make uncomfortable situations which cause fear and trepidation. The ego wants to make a deal, this for that. Spirit is continually trying to give unconditionally and that is the key to our freedom. Bargaining with the world holds us trapped in the challenges of the day. We are resident in the kingdom of heaven, right now…if we are not at peace it is because we are observing something else. Today, let us be aware, let us be observant for the things of Love, which are the things of God.

SEPTEMBER 10 – TIME – I am timeless. The linear time which we seem to be participating in is really an illusion. In our essence of Spirit, we are timeless. God is timeless and if we are to escape the continual cycle of life and death, we must realize this fact. God is the first, meaning prime…we are creations of and co-creators with God. All of creation is in the eternal now. This concept is very difficult for us to get in our minds due to the interference of the ego. We mostly are experiencing our lives through the lens of past. To further complicate things we may be anticipating the future in a fearful way, thinking that the past is the herald of the future. Stop! Take a moment right now to center yourself in the truth. God is present in this moment…we are immersed in and a part of this loving presence. There is nothing to fear in this moment. Clear away the cobwebs of the past. Release any idea of the cloudy future. This bright moment, right now is sufficient unto itself…it is the only real moment…it is eternity…timeless.

SEPTEMBER 11 – HEAL – I am healed. Take a moment right now to consider the truth of your being. We are healthy and whole, right now. There is no sickness in us. All disease is just a figment of our imagination. The body may think it is ill, but the mind can heal itself and thereby heal the body. God sees only wholeness; in this unity nothing can be out of alignment. We are on a path that will change our perception of the world and brothers and ourselves. Healing will occur as we release the conflict in our minds and embrace oneness. In the kingdom of heaven there is no inconsistency. All things work together for Good. If we perceive illness, this is surely a misperception. In the midst of the illness it is difficult to see how we can overcome it. We must raise our consciousness above the seeming condition and embrace health and wholeness, which are really the same thing. If we think that medicine will help, we should take the medicine. If we believe that the doctor has the answer, then we should see the doctor, and listen. In any event, we must begin to believe that we play a strong role in our own healing, if any of this is to be effective. Our forgiveness is healing. Physician, heal thyself.

SEPTEMBER 12 – REALITY – I am real. We are all the agents of God. God is continually creating and extending himself through us. To be true to our reality, we give love in all of our endeavors. This means letting go graven images of ourselves. We are not our jobs or even our behavior. We are children of the Light and as such we are the light itself. The true essence of us is the spirit within which lights the way before us. To be real means that we have no need of defensive postures. Truly when we are real, we cannot be harmed. Where no defense is needed, no conflict can exist. Where we have been in conflict, at last there is no conflict. There is no conflict in heaven. There is no conflict in reality.

SEPTEMBER 13 – RECOGNITION – I am recognized. God recognizes us. He knows who we are. God sees his beloved son who has never left him. Sometimes we may feel as if we have wandered far from God and the things of Good, and that we are not recognizable as part of that Good. This is erroneous thinking. God is that in which we live and move and have our being. We cannot be far from God because we are in God, always, in eternity. So, even when we cannot see, God sees. He recognizes us as his perfect creation. If we feel that we have moved away from God we can correct this thinking by centering ourselves in the spirit and visualizing that spirit extending to us, through us and as us. This is what God sees, this is what God recognizes in us...God recognizes only the good because that is all there is.

SEPTEMBER 14 – CHANGE – I am changeless. Circumstances are continually changing. The events of the world are always in flux. Situations unfold. Our existence is apparently in a constant state of change. This is just an appearance. All of this is just a veil pulled down over reality. Reality is changeless. God is changeless, the Kingdom of heaven is changeless, and I am changeless. At last we come to this…that in the timeless stretch of eternity all things already are. All living things exist and are extensions of God, life extending through God, life extending through us, life extending through our brothers. This extension is the true joy of living. Constant joy is the state of creation. Focused on eternal creation, we are at last re-integrated into the kingdom. Our willingness allows God to flow across the little, imaginary gap of separation. At last we know we are who we have always been, the people of light, the people of God. At last…

SEPTEMBER 15 – PEACE – I am at peace. Watching the news…observing the seeming chaos in the world, the ego calls us to war. This is obvious, but what is not so obvious is the fact that the ego is always calling us into conflict. We have been deprived of peace. Well, no more, let us make a commitment to peace. Today, anytime we find ourselves upset, let us release the problem through surrender and forgiveness. Let the direction of our thoughts be loving and conciliatory. The path to God is a way of peace. The way of peace is effortless being. Right now, release all conflict and feel the peace descend upon you. I am at peace, we are at peace, the world is at peace and all is well.

SEPTEMBER 16 – HOLY – I am very holy. The teacher who teaches less than this is not the one for you. Today, we are concerned with finding our true self. Truly, at the core of our being we are holy. We are like the Shamballa warriors of old, who would quietly enter the halls of those in conflict with them and remove all the weapons. We agents of the light, bringing the darkness to the light. Do not listen to the voices which say that you are less than this. The light and love of God are flowing to you, through you and as you. You are very holy and so is everyone who you contact. So, today, every meeting that we have will be a holy one. This is a holy encounter…this moment is a holy encounter. I am, you are, we are very holy.

SEPTEMBER 17 – ONE – I am undivided. Consider the first commandment. Thou shalt have one God... God is one, the oneness of God envelops us, we cannot be separate from God or from any other living thing. Whereas we have been divided, we are now aware of our unity. The practice begins with releasing any conflicts within. Let go of worries and concerns, know that you are being cared for right now. Healing the inner divisions allows us to direct this oneness out into the world. Put aside any grievances, forgive any inner hurt. We are the unified power of Love being extended into the world.

SEPTEMBER 18 – TREASURE – I am treasured. We are the treasure of God. God wants only our united return. We begin the journey back to Heaven by coming together with our brothers. As our inner strength grows we offer it to all. Consider the "prodigal son" …this is truly our story. We have travelled to a far country (in our thinking), and have riotously spent our inheritance (creative ability), and now we think we are "broke". Wanting to return home, we are welcomed, all things are given, nothing is withheld. God wants only our return, because we are God's treasure. The eternal gift of life and love are ours, it is our treasure as we are God's treasure. Let us accept our gift, and return with our brothers to the loving embrace of our Father who is in Heaven.

SEPTEMBER 19 – COMMUNICATE – I am communicating. Communications is the antidote to conflict. It is important to communicate the truth. The truth is that we are so much more than the body. The body in itself is neutral. We can use it to teach love and unity or we can use it to engage in attack. Attack is both offense and defense. Attack arises out of the perceived need to defend, because we think we may be in danger. This need to defend always turns to offense. The offense can be physical or just mental, but the results are always distress and suffering. Today, let us make a commitment to use the body as a communications device...allowing the Holy Spirit to speak through us. In this way we communicate only love.

SEPTEMBER 20 – ACTION – I am active. Living a fulfilled life, we are active in the things of Spirit. Changing our focus from getting to giving we are freed from want. Receptive to the guidance of Spirit we are always guided rightly. We are able to easily accomplish that which is ours to do. We do not need to worry about what to do or what to say, Spirit will instruct us. We will find ourselves doing proper service in all things. We will experience the sense of well-being that always accompanies love in action. We will do the right thing for the right reason at exactly the right time.

SEPTEMBER 21 – PERCEPTION – I am perceptive. Fantasy is wrong perception. In the past we may have allowed ourselves to become caught up in wishful thinking. When we wish for something to be different than what is, we are attempting to escape from our present illusion into another illusion. We are trying to be magicians, saying "poof, I want this to be that way and I want that to be this way". This is misuse of the mind. Say to yourself instead "I am one with God, and as such I am very holy." This is proper perception. When we realize our relationship with God is all there is, we have perceived correctly. When we perceive correctly, we lift up our own vision and all vision. This correct vision presents a life that reflects paradise, where there is no reason for fantasy. More importantly this vision puts us squarely on our ultimate journey and we know it.

SEPTEMBER 22 – GOD'S WILL – I am good. God's will is good. In the past we may have had some trepidation about the will of God. Perhaps we have thought that doing God's will would be a hard, spare existence. This is just not the case. God is willing only good, because that is what God is…and cannot be otherwise. To be afraid of God's will means that we must be afraid of ourselves, since we come directly from that will. God's will is not austere or painful, God's will is for life to be fully realized. We are good simply because we are creations of Good. So, today, let us will good along with God. There is no reason to fight it, we can only be frustrated in that work. The good cannot be overcome by anything, hence there is nothing to fear. We are good… we are God's Good. We are God's will.

SEPTEMBER 23 – PRAYER – I am answered. Every prayer is answered. Understand that the Holy Spirit which answers all prayer, will not give you what you don't want. If we ask for something that would cause us greater fear if it were given, it is not. Spirit will not do anything to increase fear. Your prayers have all already been answered, the answers that you are not ready to hear are still waiting for your readiness. In order to become ready, proper interaction with our brothers is needed. Today let us have faith in all those who come before us. Release all fear and concern, give only love and acceptance. Today, let us believe in God by believing in our brothers and sisters. Do not be suspicious, but rather be open. Our brothers actually come to us as answered prayer. Fear them not…your spirit can only be extended and cannot be hurt or harmed in any way. Say this (From ACIM): "Because I will to know myself, I see you as God's Son and my brother."

SEPTEMBER 24 – CORRECTION – I am correct. Correction is always just seeing rightly. You cannot really correct yourself because you are already correct (perfect). You cannot correct anyone else because they are already correct (perfect). This is sometimes hard to accept, but it is the path to peace. The ego is always checking, comparing and judging. It sees only lack and fault. True correction is the ability to heal. We heal ourselves and we heal others by seeing through and past the seeming disorder to the truth of our ultimate wholeness. Any errors that we notice are not of spirit and therefore they are illusory. Errors are corrected through forgiveness. Forgiveness means seeing it differently. Allow the Holy Spirit to show you the truth. See yourself without judgment, see others without judgment, this is correct.

SEPTEMBER 25 – HEALED – I am healed. Today, we stop trying to figure out what is wrong. That which we think is wrong is not even really there. To believe that we can be healed by understanding our illness is erroneous. Seek instead to go immediately to the truth. To believe in sin, to think that we are "sinners" is to start from an impossible position. There is no healing possible from this perspective... we can have temporary reprieve from symptoms, but new ones will appear soon. To believe we can be attacked by creation in any form is insanity. Our therapist may have told us, "Yes, the world is a dangerous place but you should not be afraid." How does this make sense? If we can be threatened, should we not put our attention on safety? If you are in danger, are we not compelled to defend? This is why we cannot escape from fear by being afraid. Spirit is gently calling us back to healing, right now. It says, you cannot be threatened, so stop threatening. All sickness falls away into the dust of non-existence as we try not to heal but rather we just let healing be.

SEPTEMBER 26 – JOY – I am joyful. Today, let us accept the joy of Spirit. It is possible to feel joy at all times and in all places. Spirit is continually sending a message of bliss. We will feel it only to the extent that we extend it to others. We are receiving unlimited blessings, in order to feel blessed we must reflect these blessings out into our experience. Miracles are happening right now…they are the healing events that return us to love. As we accept others as they are (like us), we are brought back into alignment with the Oneness of God. This is indeed atonement. Do you remember your shortcomings? You do not have any. Do you regret the errors of the past? They do not exist. Do you resent the actions of your brothers and sisters? They never happened. To experience the joy of Spirit, allow Spirit to filter and cleanse…allow Spirit to speak love to all fear.

SEPTEMBER 27 – SINGLE-MINDED – I am single-minded. Jesus says: "If thine eye be single, then thine whole body will be full of light." This is a very straight-forward instruction to clear conflict out of the mind. To see the goodness of creation in all things. God's will is our happiness, it is His will that we experience that happiness right now. The wonder and power of the universe is ours, it is our choice to accept it. It is our shared will that we realize our ultimate oneness. This may not be apparent. We may believe that we have competing visions of wellbeing. It is this competition that steals our happiness from us. Being single-minded means that we continue to return our attention to our unity whenever it seems that it does not exist. It is the ability, the discipline, to see God. The ego is afraid to do this, knowing that it will fade into the light of God. Until we come to reconcile, until we join in unity, "God Himself is incomplete..." Today, whenever the ego speaks, remember you are needed to complete God, do not listen to fear. Be single-minded, be mindful only of Good.

SEPTEMBER 28 – GRANDEUR – I am a part of the grandeur of God. Today marks the end of grandiosity. Today we choose for sinlessness, today we see one-ness, today we release the enemy and embrace the good. In the past our grandiosity has always been a cover for inadequacy. The ego knows that it is small and it attempts to hide this through grandiose fantasy. Allow the light of God to shine through this veneer of vanity. The little ego is immobilized in the "Great Rays" of heaven. It is here that we establish the veritable glow of greatness that is our inheritance. In truth we are beaming, we are a gleaming part of this grand vision of God. We are irreplaceable, nothing or no one can substitute for us with our Father. Together we comprise the Son of God. As long as we choose the ego's grandiosity, there is a gap in God…a place that goes unfilled in Creation. Jesus said: "Go forth and sin no more". This means "be perfect as your Father in Heaven is perfect." It is already so, we are perfect. We can be cleansed from the stain of sin by simply recognizing our shared grandeur. Say, to yourself right now, "I am free from sin, my brothers and sisters are free from sin."

SEPTEMBER 29 -- HOME -- I am at home. We are at home in God. We have been dreaming a fearful dream. We have forgotten that we are one and whole. We have sent ourselves into exile. Today, let us return home from our imaginary travels. Remember that we are one with God. With this in mind get comfortable and relax. Wherever we may seem to be, we are really at home in God. We are at home and safe.

SEPTEMBER 30—REMEMBER – I am remembering. I am willing to remember the truth. This remembrance is a restoration to sanity...that nothing but God exists. This is our sweetest memory. Today, let us lay aside all thoughts of defense and attack. To participate in conflict is to be in ignorance. To attack is to forget the truth. No conflict, no attack can be mounted except against ourselves. When we fight, we fight ourselves. When we give, we give to ourselves. Remember God, remember oneness.

OCTOBER

Nothing is a thing...
I mean no thing is a thing;
In order to be a thing it must
have an independent existence
and because nothing stands
alone it can't be a thing...I mean
no thing can stand alone because
everything is together.
Everything is connected.
Every thing is a part of everything.
If this seems confusing, don't worry,
it's really not a thing.

OCTOBER 1 – HEALTH – I am healthy. Spirit is sending love at all times. Take some time today to notice this healing balm. All sickness is of and begins in the divided mind. Since there is no division in reality, then there really is no sickness. Illness is just another cry for love…it is asking for the love that we believe is not present. The focus on sickness has become an idol…something to be devoted to. The idol of illness is self-centered, self-created and self-destructive. Being a false substitute, illness is just a deceiver. It is just a symbol of our call for that comfort that we think we have lost. Spirit can heal this craziness right now…why not ask?

OCTOBER 2 – PEACE – I am peaceful. There can be no peace in fear. There can be no peace in any outer acquisition. Nothing dragged in from the "outside" can make us whole. It is erroneous to believe that we are incomplete. Our peace truly lies in the reality that we are already whole and complete. There is an altar within us, we have obscured it but we can remove the veil right now. This is the altar to the One God. Always available, always accessible this is our retreat from the madness of division. Here at the center of peace we can worship. Peace is on the inside, and only inside can we find it. We can become peaceful.

OCTOBER 3 – RICH – I am rich. We are already rich. All of the abundance of the universe is ours...it is our inheritance. As Son of God we are the heirs to the kingdom of Heaven. This means that we inherit all that there is! This state of plenty can never be taken from us. No worries...no problem...no crisis can deplete the store of riches that are already in our name. Consider this truth...notice that as fear of lack retreats, inspiration increases...a way is made in the wilderness...a path to ultimate prosperity is clear. We are rich.

OCTOBER 4 – ETERNAL – I am eternal. Lately we have seen a great rush to anti-aging technology. Some of this seems attractive and by no means do we want to suggest that we should ignore the ongoing health of the body. However, it is important to remember that in spirit we are already eternal and it is not necessary to obsess over the mortality of the body. This is just another idol. We are first and foremost eternal, ever-living spirit. We are loved not for our striving but for who we are at our essence. This eternal love cannot be bargained for, bought or traded. All of our attempts to do so merely block our awareness of that same love. We are eternal and we are eternally loved.

OCTOBER 5 – FAITH – I am faithful. So often we have put our faith in idols…idols and demons. We have pursued money and possessions but they have not comforted us. Medicines have fallen short of curing us. Oh, we allay the temporary symptoms, but some form of the sickness always returns. Prestige, influence and "being liked" have not fulfilled us. Our faith in these surface things has failed us. Stop thinking about these illusions, release them, let them go. The love of God within us is the answer to all trouble. The love God which extends to us becomes the solution to all suffering as we allow this love to extend from us. Let us have faith in God, let us have faith in our brothers and sisters.

OCTOBER 6 – MIND – I am a part of the mind of God. We dwell in the mind of God. The mind of God is infinite, which means that it has no end. So, we are intimately involved in this. To be alone means that we would have to separate from infinity, this is impossible. There can be none outside of the limitless which by definition has no limits. God is without beginning and without end. Today, let us stop excluding ourselves from the universe. Get a sense of inclusion…this is our home, eternal and unchanging. Jesus said "I and my Father are one" the message is We and the Father are one. We are part of the mind of God.

OCTOBER 7 – UNDERSTANDING – I am understanding. From time to time during this day there will be many opportunities for understanding to grow. Foundationally we must understand that God stands under all. God is the foundation upon which all things stand. Distress, upset, anger, sickness all of these are denial of the underlying unity of all life. Healing these disorders are just lessons in understanding. Understanding is compassion and compassion is love and love is the substance of good. When my brother seems to be at odds with me, I must understand that he is simply asking for love. This may not be apparent, but it is none the less true. When my body seems to be sick, I must understand that this is also a call of love and that the apparent symptoms are not real. The cure for the disorders in my relationships and in my body are the same. Understanding allows me to move past these delusions and into the solution which is always the extension of the love to God…through me and out to all of creation.

OCTOBER 8 – CHOICE – I am choosing. Today and every day we choose how our lives will be. We choose between darkness and light. If we feel tired, we have exhausted ourselves. If we are hurting, we have injured ourselves. Suffering is not of God. We can choose again. The peace of God is surrounding us at all times. There is within us the still, soft voice…this is the voice for God. It is quiet, being without conflict. Conflict strikes out in all directions because it does not see. Attack brings darkness to the attacker, reconciliation brings light. Which would we rather have? It really is our choice. Where we have known pain, we can have bliss. There is a clear path to joy, it is not hard it is just a change. We are the people of the light and as such we walk in the light. Get out of the alley, get out of the dark. Abide in the light, extend the light, choose the light, be the light.

OCTOBER 9 – HEIR – I am heir. We are heir to the kingdom. Any time we are feeling deprived, we should realize that we have deprived ourselves. Sometimes it may seem as if the world is conspiring against us. Circumstances may appear to be stealing our good from us. Our brothers may look to be in competition with us. Be assured that all of this is an illusion. We are heir to the goodness of God and nothing or no one can steal it from us, we can only take it from ourselves. The answer is sharing...in sharing the abundance freely, we gain immeasurably. As we share we are all glorified. We bask in the glory of God, which is to say in the light of heaven. Such is our inheritance; let us not accept anything less.

OCTOBER 10 – STRENGTH – I am strong in spirit. The will of God is our power and our strength. There is no weakness in us. The ego continues to complain about how put upon we are...ignore it. Look at it for what it is, a delusional thought system and then put it and its opinion aside. All real strength comes from our connection to God and it is more than enough to accomplish everything that we need to do. We are independent in our ability to create, but all of our creation is dependent on God, and interdependent with the rest of creation (our brothers). We are completely dependent on God for our very existence, but we are also sharing our function with God. This is the most marvelous thing, and indeed it is the essence of our being. We are strong in Spirit.

OCTOBER 11 – REDEMPTION – I am redeemed. It is easy to believe that we have sinned and so have put ourselves outside the grace of God. The ego continues to call our behavior and the behavior of our brothers into question. It is a good thing that we are not our behavior. Our actions in the world are nothing but a reflection of our attitudes and beliefs. If we are acting out of fear, what occurs is suffering...but it is not an indication of our true value and worth. It is a cover for the fear and sense of conflict that is naturally present in ego. If we are acting in love, what occurs is joy...which is an indication of our true value and worth. Whichever path we choose today will determine our experience. In any case we are not condemned. Because our value and worth are always the same, we cannot be stained. We can only, by our own choice, delay our return to love. We are redeemed by the love of God which is our own true love.

OCTOBER 12 – SOLUTION – I am in the solution. To be in the solution rather than the problem, this is a common saying of the day. We hear "Stay in the solution". This most commonly seems to mean to focus on a positive attitude and working through to a desirable end. Today, let us look deeper than this. First, we should ask ourselves a question: "What do I want? The problem or the answer." We really only have one problem and that is our self-centeredness. This problem has been described in many ways: separation, division, conflict, judgment, self-consciousness, selfishness, loneliness…all of these are just different aspects of the same thing. There is only one solution…and that solution is One. Whenever a problem appears, the solution is always present. Being in the solution really means being in love. To stay in the solution means to keep our mind stayed on love. Focused on the fact that we made of love and that we just need to extend that which we are made of out into the problem. This will always be the solution and it is always available. We are in the solution and the solution is in us.

OCTOBER 13 – HELP – I am helpful. We are learning to release anger and extend love. Every loving thought is a blessing…only loving thoughts are worthy of the Son of God. Today, let us focus on giving that which we are asked to give. If someone seems to be in conflict with us, the conflict will be healed by our ability to return to love. There is no justification to anger and anytime we find ourselves angry it will be because we have misinterpreted the evidence. We have seen a threat where none exists. We have misjudged. The seeming offense was just a request for help. Our practice should be to apply healing to all hurts, to extend love to all lack, and to be at one with our adversary. What this means is that every time we seem to be attacked, it is really just another opportunity to give of ourselves. Let us give help to those who ask…let us be helpful.

OCTOBER 14 – REMEMBER – I am enlightened. We already have all knowledge; we just can't access it in the midst of ego. Our study in the workings of harmony is a device to recall our memories of God. I become sick because I do not love myself. Because I do not love myself I am continually calling for that love. I do this in a variety of ways, only one of which is the apparent illness. Healing comes from remembering the truth. Healing will come directly from my request for enlightenment. Whenever I feel disconnected in any way, whether it is a disagreement with a brother or an illness, the path to wholeness begins with a request for knowledge. So, today, I will ask Holy Spirit to continually supply me with the proper perspective so that I might be able to bridge the gap to true knowledge.

OCTOBER 15 – SEEKING – I am seeking. We have been looking for love in all the wrong places. This misperception is the cause of all of our unhappiness and pain. We have believed that we will be fulfilled through gaining the respect and acceptance of others. We have believed that others opinion of us is of overriding importance. We have been looking outside of ourselves for salvation. We have tried to drag the things of the material world inside to fill us up. No more! Today, let us seek the truth. We can know the peace of God if we just seek it. If we really want to be healthy and whole, we simply stop striving to increase ourselves from the outside and begin to increase ourselves by extending ourselves to life. We seek the way of love and that is surely the path to peace.

OCTOBER 16 – SANITY – I am sane. Love is unified, in its unification lies its strength. It cannot be split and so it is whole (sane). Sanity means being whole and undivided. Insanity is the result of the split mind...which in turn has us viewing the world as fragmented. Alone, in our ego, we are unable to learn the truth, we need continual guidance from this power which is greater than the ego in order to be restored to sanity. Self-taught we remain self-deluded. Today we need to open ourselves totally to the teaching of Spirit. We have limitless potential when we are able to let go of our delusional thought system. Our teacher stands ever ready to inform us, let us give ourselves over to the one great mentor...spirit within. Sanity returns as oneness is acknowledged. Say to yourself, I am sane.

OCTOBER 17 – VISION – I am visionary. I am envisioning my life. In the past we may have had a vision of some level of abundance which when achieved would free us from worry. This is the ego twisting the truth. The truth is that we already have all that there is, because at our core, at our source we are all that there is. We are an integral part of creation and as such part of God. The ego is making promises of riches in the world. It would trade these outer things for our soul. This is impossible and cannot really happen but we have made the deal anyway. Selling our soul is really not possible, but we think we have done it, thus the guilt and illness follows. Spirit is working to heal this incorrect perception and to uncover true vision. True vision shows us the truth of God's love, which is the Christ in us and in our brothers.

OCTOBER 18 – WITHIN – I am looking within. Today, let us make a commitment to stop looking to outer things for our salvation. That new job, new house, new car, new relationship is not our salvation. We may enjoy job, house, car, or relationship only to the extent that we realize that they do not complete us because we are already complete. In this regard we can see that we are complete without them, and they are just a "bonus". Contrary to mainstream Christian doctrine, Jesus is not going to "come into us". The spirit that was in Jesus is already within us. All we have to do is turn our attention to it. Nothing from the outside is going to fill us because nothing outside exists. It is just an illusion. Let us look within, for it is there that the answer lies.

OCTOBER 17 – ATTRACTION – I am attracting love. The answer of course is love. If the answer is love, then what is the question? It does not matter because regardless of the question, the answer is love. Miracles are the sign that we are attracting love into our experience. We have a role to play in the healing of the world. Our mind is split; we see the world as split. As we forgive every appearance of division, we are really healing the world. We are bringing the various fragments back into wholeness. Every healing act attracts more love into our lives. Every attack attracts more fear into our lives. We attract that which we seek. That which we seek is always found. If we seek the verification of threat, we will attract illness…mental and physical. Fear and violence will be the result. Let us change our approach, let us seek that which we really want …peace, let us knock on the door of harmony and it will be opened.

OCTOBER 18 – INNOCENT – I am innocent. We are innocent. If we are innocent, then why do we feel so guilty? We feel guilty because we believe that we have left God; and that further we have caused the death of God's Son; at some level we have come to the conclusion that we have actually killed God and usurped the Throne. This is the basic cause of all discomfort...it is the underlying reason for all suffering. It is the ultimate in self-centeredness. This monumental guilt is so uncomfortable that in order for us to escape it, we project it out into the world that we see. In another words, we attack. We only attack because we feel guilty. We feel guilty because we have separated ourselves from our brothers. Seeing our brothers and sisters as being apart from us, we perceive that they are a threat to us. Having judged them, we condemn them. This is all delusion. In truth we are innocent and so are all of our brothers. Let us make an attempt, today to bring our consciousness back into harmony with all of life.

OCTOBER 19 – BORN – I am born again. Being born again means that we have had a change of mind. Where once we considered ourselves at the mercy of cruel fate. We are becoming aware of the goodness that God has for us. We believed that we were born into suffering. Our lives may have seemed to just continue to expand into more pain. Sadness followed more sadness. Death seemed to be lurking just out of sight. We felt deserted and then we deserted others. This is the life ego has chosen for us...a life that leads only to grim and certain death. We are not sentenced to this continuous cycle of birth and death. We can short circuit this madness by waking up to eternity. Revelation is the only birth that will bring us back into reality. Life is ours and it is ours always.

OCTOBER 20 – PICTURE – I am a picture of wholeness. We are a picture of health and wholeness. The kingdom of Heaven is wellbeing…this is in contrast to the world we have seen. In that world we perceive crucifixion…the continual threat of and eventual punishment for mistakes. God's son cannot be punished except by his own hand and even then it is only illusion. Why do we accept suffering when we can have bliss? Picture health, picture wholeness and be happy. Guilt keeps us from this picture, but we can release it right now. As soon as we choose love, guilt will disappear and then we will be whole indeed.

OCTOBER 21 – JOURNEY – I am on a journey. The ego has set us upon a trip that can never find home. On the ego's mission We will continue to wander aimlessly from one fix to another, never finding any true satisfaction. This is totally unnecessary, for God has set a divine appointment with us, that cannot be missed. Spirit has put us upon a journey that will bring us home, where our Father awaits our return. Today let us discontinue our freakish trip into self-centeredness…let us pick up the yoke of light and get on with our true mission…our journey back to God.

OTCOBER 22 – REDEMPTION – I am redeemed. Redemption is simply freedom from fear. There are only two thought systems, thoughts of love and thoughts of fear. The fear system is a knot of misbeliefs that has us thinking we are in conflict with those and around us and indeed, with life itself. Death and destruction seem imminent and inescapable. Fear, in a nutshell, says lack...it preaches the religion of hate...the pursuit of the desires of the ego at all costs. These thoughts are insane thoughts, they are sick and they are of sickness. Thoughts of love are eternal, and also expanding...they are our gift to our Self. In love we are rich, because we already have all of the gifts of creation at our beck and call. We are able to bring about paradise on earth and assure eternal paradise in the present moment. This is redemption...this is healing and this is sanity.

OCTOBER 23 – ETERNITY – I am present. We have recently been trapped in the past...we may believe that we are still there. Eternity is not just an endless succession of one moment following another, one event after another... eternity is just the present. The present is now, and it is always. Sometimes in the quiet of meditation we have touched this eternity. A quiet assurance comes over us and we are aware of the inter-connection of all living things. We know that we are in the presence of Creation and that all is well. Time stops...our perception of time comes to a halt. We exist as we always have in the bosom of our Loving Parent, at peace and in harmony. Do not listen to the voice of ego which is calling you into the past. Resist the temptation to look back...stay right here, right now, in eternity.

OCTOBER 24 – WISDOM – I am wise. Wisdom seems to be an interim stage along the road from perception to knowledge. What we perceive seems to be reality. We see a world of pain and suffering and we believe that it is our fault, or that it is our brothers fault. The beginning of wisdom will be the day that we realize that our physical vision is faulty, that our interpretation of events in is error and that our reaction to these misjudgments is further cause for more misjudgment. We are wise when we stop and ask spirit to interpret what we see and show us the truth. The more often we do this, the closer we move to our ultimate destination. Spirit will continue to inform us and it will move our perception to the place where we can come back into contact with God and then will not just be wise, we will know.

OCTOBER 25 – ARISE – I am free. We are free, we have risen from death. There is no death…this is the truth of our being. Oh, yes, the body can die. This is disturbing because we think the body is us…it is not. We are light beings. We are children of God, children of Light. Jesus showed us in the resurrection that death cannot hold us. Although it is not Easter season, let us consider that message. The Easter story is our story…we have been persecuted in our thinking, we have been pursued by phantoms of our imagination, and finally we have been crucified by the shadows of our perception. The past has chased us into the future and then caused our demise…all is as has been planned by the ego. This is illusion…let us rise in consciousness…let us rise as Jesus did, into reality. We are free, we have risen.

OCTOBER 26 – HAPPY – I am happy. Spirit fills me with joy. The smile on my face shows that I am enjoying the moment, but the spark of life in my eyes is evident to everyone that I am filled with happiness. This joy does not come from any outer circumstance. It is inside job; it is the elation that comes from my relationship with God. No matter what happens to me or around me, I stay the course. I am upbeat and positive. I know that I can do all things and weather all storms because I have a buoy of happiness that is constantly uplifting me. Creation is the source of my gladness. My life is rich and growing richer because that spirit is being expressed through me. Today I am the harbinger of joy, it comes with me and moves out to embrace the others in my life. My smile is the happy introduction, but my eyes are the genuine messengers, delivering love directly from my joy-filled soul.

OCTOBER 27 – ATONEMENT – I am at one. Today let us find our lost unity. Our oneness is present always, we have just misplaced it. There is a presence within us that is in constant contact with the unity of all life…that is the Holy Spirit…our connection with our true Self. Spirit leads us and knows the path we need to follow; in ego we have been lost. Today let us pay attention to inner guidance, giving trust where it is needed. As we learn to accept our brothers as they are we return to harmony with them. This is our function in the world, to forgive the appearance of evil, to embrace good and extend love. As we give to life, we are rewarded with awareness of our oneness with life. Share love with those who live in loneliness and escape with them intact.

OCTOBER 28 – LIGHT – I am the light. The quiet light of Spirit lives in us. The light is totally open and unguarded. All things are revealed in this light, nothing can be hidden. No shadows remain to hide fearful things. No past event, no dark projection can stand in opposition to this light. Even death must fade into nothingness in the face of this ultimate love. Let us decide for the light. Release all thought of conflict and allow healing to reign. In the light we are in perfect communication with Life. Where previously we have barred the gates let us throw them open so that God can welcome us into the temple that lies deep within us.

OCTOBER 29 – REFLECT – I am a reflection of holiness. We are holy, we were created holy, and this cannot be changed by any opinion to the contrary. Today, let us offer up our ego…our personality to God that it might be set right. Where we may have thought to keep secrets we now see that they hold us in suffering. How much better to become a mirror for heaven, a reflection of the Great Rays. We need clean the mirror of all other aspirations, lest they become idols that keep us from attaining our long sought goal. The reflection of God shining through us will bring us all to wholeness. This aspect of holiness in us is the very picture of holiness. Let it shine forth to heal the world.

OCTOBER 30 – EQUAL – I am equal. We are all ultimately equal in the kingdom of heaven. As we are equal, so also are the miracles that bring us into awareness of the kingdom. There is no competition in giving. We give to all who come before us because that is what is called for. There is no need in to appear grand; the concern for appearance will actually hide the good in the shadows of ego. The only concern we need have in the working of miracles is the free gift or in answer of the call for a gift. Be aware that when a brother comes asking, it is our honor to answer our equal with love. When we are not responding to a request we must continue to shine the miracle working power of love to all life. Equal in love, is equal in all.

OCTOBER 31 – TRUTH – I am truthful. Today, we will live the truth. As a fragment, our power is diminished and obscured. Let us tell no tales which further weaken our lives. Observe the truth and let it then be known. As we may have noticed seeming flaws in our character, and then projected them out into others we can also see that the goodness which resides in us also lives in our kinship. The truth is that the flaws are simply distractions which keep us from focusing on the true image. In ego we cannot understand we must simply react. We can remember however that any time we feel disturbed that we have simply lost the thread of true consciousness and must ask spirit to reinterpret that which appears upsetting. Do this now, release the past and embrace the power of the present moment. Be truthful…

NOVEMBER

Ego desire
Fights me
For sanity;
Wants to own,
To grasp and
Hold that
Which cannot
Be taken but
Only given.
A moment
Of clarity
Shines away
The fear
Revealing the
Pure heart's
Desire for
Oneness.

NOVEMBER 1 – QUIET – I am quiet. Today we release all of the distractions that keep us from knowing the peace of God. Take a moment right now to center yourself. Feel the presence of Spirit that is both within you and all around you. Visualize yourself without any worries or concerns… what does this feel like? What does it mean to you to release all anxiety? Go ahead and let go right now. The lessons learned in this quiet place are the only ones worth learning… for they are the lessons of spirit. These are the classes that change our perspective to the point that we can actually come to true knowledge. Time is a device in which we can learn the lessons of the Holy Spirit or we can continue to entertain the ego. Today, let us decide for peace.

NOVEMBER 2 – SURE – I am sure. We can be free from doubt, but we must will that it be so. As we move through the world, we will notice how limited we seem to be in ordering our own lives. We will witness how inadequate our brothers seem to be in ordering theirs or in helping us, even a little bit. This is the ego distracting us with the tricks of time…references to the past and projections into the future. Be sure that these are all illusions. Free yourself from any doubt that you exist in eternity. Forgive your own shortcomings, by seeing that they are just mistakes and that they can be corrected. Forgive the appearance of defects in your brother by seeing the inner Christ. Trust your brother and trust in your Self. Be sure that this is Truth.

NOVEMBER 3 – MAGNIFICENT – I am magnificent? We are magnificent...together we accomplish Heaven. Alone we find our small selves in hell. Our littleness is the ego's pursuit of the things of world...it is the thought that we will feel better if just had this or that thing. This is such a weak and pitiful goal, that it is not worthy of us. All of this striving is just substitution. We long for the golden light of Heaven, but we settle for the tarnished gates of Mitzeraim (Egypt). At our core we a magnificent...we have all of the potential of the universe in us. Just a change of focus will bring us into awareness of our magnitude. Attend to the things of God...bringing love and service to all whom we meet. Then we will see our true role and we will also experience unlimited prosperity.

NOVEMBER 4 – HOLY INSTANT – I am in the Holy Instant. God wills good and that good is right now. We have heard it said "In God's time not mine" …meaning that sometime later God will give us his blessing. This is an upside down idea. There is no need to wait for our Good. God is offering it to us right now…all of our praying, begging really for some good thing to come to us is in vain…all of God's good is available to us right now…in the Holy Instant. All we have to do is recline into it. Let all smallness go. Release all schemes into the arms of the Holy Spirit. Here again is the call for willingness, your mind does not have to be empty, you just need to be willing to release the little thoughts that reside there. Spirit will not fight your wishes, but it will help you recognize what you really want. Get in the moment, God is waiting.

NOVEMBER 5 – RELATE – I am relating. We are in relationship to all living things. The web of life connects us. We are already whole and complete, being part of creation we cannot be otherwise. Let us take this day for reflection on the value of our brothers and sisters. We may believe that we need certain of them to act in such a way so that we may feel better. We may think that we must keep people in their various roles. This is like putting people on the shelf… when we want them we take them down from there to play with them and then put them back when we are done. This will never be truly satisfying. Allow the spirit to inform the body, see God everywhere. Extend love to everyone in your life and communicate nothing else.

NOVEMBER 6 – ATTRACTION – I am attracted to Spirit. True attraction is the magnetism of life to life. Today let the Holy Spirit release your vision, so that you might see correctly. As you do this notice how the light begins to grow brighter all around you. There is a shift of consciousness which will allow you to see the light in all of those who you meet today. You will be attracted to their spirit…which is of God. Make a decision to use the body only to communicate love. No more attack, but rather reconciliation.

NOVEMBER 7 – CHRIST – I am in Christ. "Let the mind that was in Christ Jesus be in you." This is not some magical minded incantation in which we ask some presence from without to come within to give us a blessing. This is a straight instruction for us to think with the same mind as Christ…this mind is already within us; all we have to do is allow ourselves to share its thoughts. This is divine mind which we share with all of creation. Perhaps Paul did not understand this fully, but he knew enough to recognize that the consciousness that was in Jesus was something different than that which was normal. He saw that this higher state of mind was also highly desirable. Let us pay attention to this, we are in the Christ mind and the Christ mind is in us.

NOVEMBER 8 – HARMONY – I am in harmony. Distracted by the things of the world, we sometimes feel as if we are of two minds. Our higher Self is calling us to our best...our smallness is promising some fleeting gift in exchange for our attention. Today, let us harmonize our mind...let go of smallness and embrace the grand vision of Heaven. Whenever anxiety comes today, tell yourself: "The solution to this division comes from my higher Self." Relax into the presence of Love and know that you are being cared for. There is no division, we are all one with the One, and the thoughts of this one Mind are ours to use. We are in harmony.

NOVEMBER 9 – SPIRIT – I am spirit. This is the end of conflict...focusing on the fact that we are spirit lets us know that we cannot be alone and that all are spirit. Holiness lies in us; it is our deepest reality. We are all part of God, unlimited in our abilities. We are safe and cannot be threatened. Healing comes instantly to all ills, we are whole. We are free...we can choose the forgiveness that forgets all grievances. Every time we accept this truth, spirit is fed and we are all made stronger. We are one, we are free in spirit.

NOVEMBER 10 – DEDICATE – I am dedicated. Today we dedicate ourselves to Goodness. We take sides on the only side there really is...Truth. All argument falls away as we see that Truth cannot be contradicted. Dedicate this moment to congress with Creation...communicate your love to everything...right now. Each of us has a part to play in healing the world and our part may sometimes involve taking action, but our part always involves extending love to whatever situation we think needs it. Extend love first and then consider what action is required. Throughout the day, whenever you feel assailed by circumstances or events, stop and remember your dedication to Truth. Say to yourself: "I accept my role in the healing of the world."

NOVEMBER 11 – FUNCTION – I am functioning. Our function is to forgive the world we see. God's will is always for good, it really is the best and highest for all concerned. This means that whenever something is not good, it cannot be God's will. If it is not God's will then it really does not exist. Why then do we see it? We see ill when we become lost in self-centered separation from creation. We may correct this misperception simply be practicing our function…the forgive the world we see. God is love and all that does not show that love is a "sin" that we need to forgive. God does not forgive it because to Him it has never existed. We have made it, let us heal it in the present moment. Healing and forgiveness are the same. Our function then is to heal…to forgive…

NOVEMBER 12 – ESSENTIAL – I am essential. We complete God's creation, without us there is a gap in Heaven. We are essential to the wellbeing of the universe. When we become lost in our self-centeredness God misses us. He calls to us through Spirit, gently asking our return. God's will for us is bliss. We can choose this for ourselves right now. We do not have to wait until some future time, let us just release any other thought that seems to be occupying our mind. Let go of all other goals, and embrace the goal of God's will. We can align ourselves with Goodwill right now. Ease and comfort will surely follow. Centered in the light of God, we relax into our role. We heal the fracture in the cosmos by flowing into it.

NOVEMBER 13 – SHARE – I am sharing God's happiness. Whenever we share the light of Creation with any other, we come together in that light. It grows brighter and stronger… we are made whole in it and together we are happy. Suffering does not accomplish anything but suffering, even this though, Spirit can use to bring about a new state of mind. Where we have believed that strife somehow will bring a reward, we begin to see that the reward is God's happiness which is always present and available for us. Sharing God's will is to love the one you are with…give love and have bliss. Today, let us put our attention on happiness, let us share it and let us spread it to everyone we meet.

NOVEMBER 14 – HAPPY – I am happy. There is no love without happiness…the idea of a sad love is only a remnant of grievance. There is no space where the love of God does not exist, so there is no place where happiness is not. Choose happiness in place of sadness. Choose love instead of fear. Today, we can release all fear of God…God is our father and He has nothing but love for us. To fear God is to be afraid of joy. Why would we fear joy? Obviously it is an error and needs to be corrected. Do it now…realize the presence and power of Good that exists in you. Revel in this sense of oneness and then begin to extend it out to all that you perceive. Notice how this exercise heals hurts and frees us from concern. Don't worry…be happy.

NOVEMBER 15 – EMPATHY – I am empathetic – Watching the news, listening to reports we will find many reasons to be concerned. We may feel like the suffering described is our own suffering. We need not share in this pain. True empathy is recognizing the pain and then linking with others in an effort to see the alleviation of it. In this way we see ultimate bliss for them and for us. The holy spirit is in us, guiding us to proper service…Spirit does not see suffering and does not understand it…we can do likewise. Give joy for apparent suffering by refusing to make the suffering real. Know that our brothers and sisters are not, in reality, harmed. They are in the kingdom of God right now even as are we. Let us know this truth and thereby free ourselves and the rest of us.

NOVEMBER 16 – HOLINESS – I am very holy. We are holy...in our coming together we have the power of holiness. The insane ego says "beware, you are alone and unprotected." This is fragmentation and it is the ego's great agenda. This is truly mental illness, but to the ego it is quite practical. This twisted thinking ensures its survival. We are instruments of miracles; we are the agents of love in our lives. We cannot and do not work alone. Spirit is always with us, strengthening us and connecting us with life. Today, we can relax into spirit not worrying about how we will do our part. In this quietness we gather the strength and we are enlightened...without effort we will extend our holiness. We will connect with those around us and observe the light of God in all of us.

NOVEMBER 17 – TEACHER – I am teaching. We are all teaching, all the time. We teach lessons of fear or we teach benefits of love. It is neither important nor helpful to call people's apparent shortcomings to their attention. It is however quite beneficial to recognize the good in others and teach them that. In this way all are raised higher in consciousness. We can decide today what we will reinforce... truth or lies. Let us teach only love, giving that which is called for in all situations. As we offer this example, we are ministers of God and teachers of Heaven.

NOVEMBER 18 – REALITY – I am real. We are in reality when we can observe the unity of all life. We are real in the light of Good. Today let us release the illusion that the apparent behavior of others determines our wellbeing. We can let go of the hate which we harbor. Examine the reality…there is no reason to expect anyone to act the way we think we need them to act. First it relegates them to a role and makes them an object. Second it ties our happiness to the actions of the figments of our imagination. This is the truth, when we believe that others are either a threat to us or our protection against the dangers of the world they are not real, they are just shadows we have created in the darkness of self-centeredness. Be real, be reconciled with life.

NOVEMBER 19 – UNION – I am unified. Holding onto levels of relationships keeps us all in bondage. It may seem natural to have stronger feelings for some people in our lives than for some others. These strong feelings can appear to be either good or bad. We have good feelings for those we think are closer to us. We have bad feelings for those who we discern are a threat to us. We hold those around us hostage to our own delusional whims. We will do well to recognize the only difference in these relationships is how we perceive the past behavior of each person. Given time we will move them from one category to another, and we probably are already entertaining multiple categories. This is the division of relationship and it is false. The truth is we are unified, we are a part of all and all are a part of us.

NOVEMBER 20 – COMPLETE – I am complete. We are complete…but sometimes we are feeling much less than this. Heaven is our goal and in fact we have already attained it…we have only dreamed that we have left it. Our practice now is to come back into awareness. We really do not have to anything but surrender to the presence of Spirit within us. If we find our thoughts straying to conflict, let us be willing to let Spirit cleanse us. The tiniest portion of willingness on our part will link to the great power that is always present in us. We will see our completeness and then will be comforted and at ease. So, today, let us just relax into peace of mind and allow that Mind to guide us to oneness.

NOVEMBER 21 – FORGIVE – I am forgiving. Forgiveness is letting go of the past. Letting go of the past frees us from all conflict. It is only by focusing on the past that we can hold on to misery. In the present, in the Holy Moment there is naught but bliss. Love lives in and through us in eternity, it cannot exist in our thoughts when we are attracted to a past occurrence or when we are projecting into an uncertain future. Forgiveness happens when we forget past hurts, when we choose love instead of fear. Anger flees in the face of God's goodness. The light of Creation dissipates the shadows of fragmentation. As we forgive we are healed and we heal all of those whom we have held in the bondage of guilt and shame. Let us release these nightmarish demons right now and come into harmony with all of our brothers and sisters.

NOVEMBER 22 – WILLING – I am willing. The beginning of willingness is the opening for Truth to enter. We can be so attached to the material world that it is difficult to let go. All of our life experiences are potential for distraction. Holding on to false evidence hinders us in our search. Only ask for guidance and it will be delivered. Stop trying to do anything on your own. Nothing real is accomplished out of the personality...alone we can do nothing. Literally all of our personal reactions to the events of the day are nothing but continued attempts to find division in a world of harmony. Today, let us align our will with Goodwill... let us decide with God.

NOVEMBER 23 – TRANSFORM – I am transformed. The Holy Spirit is charged with transforming our perceptions. The great transformer is in us and always operating for our benefit. He offers light for darkness. A path out of fear and anger is available to us at every moment of every day. Just relax, release, and let go. Ease into the company of your brothers, relax into Spirit. Be open to the gifts that are present for you and release any expectations. Forgive the past and let go of any worry for the future. Transformation is really just remembering. Let us attempt to recall the truth… the real world is here and it is now…just obscured by the shadows. The light of God is already shining for us. Let us turn our attention to the wonder of that Truth.

NOVEMBER 24 – LIGHT – I am in the light. Today we will attempt to come out of the shadows. Truly forgiveness is remembering only love, and forgetting everything else. Every time we meet someone we have an opportunity to forgive. People we think we know present our past experiences to us, people we think we don't know show us dark future possibilities. Of course, both are the same, just seen from different perspectives…both are wraiths…shadows drawn over reality. It is our ego that generates the shadows…little replicas of itself which it then projects onto others. Take a moment now, allow the light that shines within to come forth. Notice how the light in you dissipates the shadows you have gathered around you. This cleanses our brothers and us…restoring us to our true state…the state of love and light.

NOVEMBER 25 – HEALED – I am healed. We are healed in the love of God. Salvation has become such a charged word; all sorts of strange religious connotations abound in regards to it. Some very weird ideas have come forth in relation to it. Salvation literally means safety, it connotes health and wholeness. It cannot be purchased because it is already ours. It cannot be taken from us. because it is integral to who we are and cannot be divided from us. It also cannot be realized alone. Salvation is a group activity so to speak. We cannot experience it alone. This means the idea of personal salvation is erroneous, salvus comes from oneness. When the many become One we are saved. No one can be left behind. When we are reconciled with our fellows we come back into awareness of God and we are all healed.

NOVEMBER 26 – CLEAR – I am clear. Today we look past circumstances and see the truth. Holy Spirit is continually trying to return us to the kingdom of heaven. Spirit's purpose is simple, strip away all of the lies we have told ourselves and reveal the reality beyond our perception. To link our purpose to our Teacher's purpose is to hurry our happy return Home. So let us be clear in our intentions. Things happen and then we try to figure out what it meant… and we are generally wrong. Begin with the end in mind. Every situation we find ourselves in can be an opportunity to practice our purpose. If we hold our goal of unity in mind, we can accomplish it moment by moment.

NOVEMBER 27 – FAITH – I am faithful. Today, let us stop accepting substitutes for what we really want. Faith is our perceiving faculty. It is our ability to see past the apparent details our suffering and know the truth. Here is the reality, at home and at peace, we are part of life and as such part of God. Every apparent situation is relational. All of this life is about relationships, relationships with other people and ideas. It is all just one thing after another…one distraction after another…we are missing the truth because we are using these distractions to keep us from uncovering the highest reality, which is what faith is for…to see through the darkness and into the light.

NOVEMBER 28 – INSTANT – I am in the instant. The instant is eternity. Creation exists only in the present. The past is gone; the future never will be. Today, let us commit to bringing our attention into the present moment. The more intention we put into keeping our attention in the moment the closer we come to the holy instant. To be released from depression, sickness, pain and darkness… that is the function of the moment. To actually live in the present means that we are free from the past. In the moment we have no reason to attack, we have no problems that plague, we have no worries or fears. In the moment we are God's children, whole and free…in the moment we are together and therefore we are saved.

NOVEMBER 29 – ROLE – I am unconditional. Today, we will stop putting people into categories. Being confused, thinking that people are provided for our own gratification is not helpful. We must closely examine our tendency to assign roles to our brothers and sisters. Every relationship that we have can lend itself to this sort of control and projection. If we desire peace, we will stop judging one against another. We will begin to see that we are all of equal value and that our value lies in our true identity, not in what we do or don't do. We are all connected in the vast web of life and each of us has a true task to accomplish, let us get out of the way so our brother may accomplish his work and that we may do likewise. To give unconditional, proper service to others is the highest aspiration that we can hold. Let us release any other goal. Give all to have all. No more comparing, see only equality and unity…be unconditional.

NOVEMBER 30 – DREAM – I am waking. Let us attempt a small awakening today. In the past we may have thought it pleasant to live in a fantasy world where magic acts to bring about our wishes and desires. At first look this seems desirable, a paradise…but looking more closely we find that our fantasies generally involve anger, revenge, and the control of others. Consider the news of the day…whatever disaster which we watch unravel, we have conflicting opinions about what should be done. We feel powerless to do anything, so we begin to fantasize about punishment for those involved. We may see some utopian vision of how the world could be if our values were somehow foisted upon everyone else. Let us stop this self-aggrandized dream. Let go the hostages of our dark vision and see the situation in the light of God. Give it to Spirit to correct our seeing and that will allow true healing, in ourselves and in all others.

DECEMBER

Christmas moon

Oh, can you
See it?
For a moment,
Out from behind
a cloud here.
Looking, now
I can only
Think of my
Love for you;
Wonderful and
Huge on
The horizon,
Then seems to
Shrink as
It rises but
Still as large
And as bright
In my heart.

DECEMBER 1 – LIGHT – I am in the light. We are on the brink…in the twisted reality of our fantasies we stand on the brink of great victory or great defeat it all depends upon the perspective. Of course the perspective changes as fear changes its aspects from vanity to covetousness. This brinksmanship, however exciting, is not in our best interest. We see trouble and problems and pain, we could see peace and love and oneness. In the light there is only the presence and power of God. All other evidence to the contrary is false evidence. Let go of fear today, take your brothers hand (at least in your consciousness), walk together in the light and see clearly how all of the errors of the past and the concerns for the future are washed away in the great flood of God's love.

DECEMBER 2 – WILLING – I am willing. Again, it is willingness that is necessary. It is all that is required for great change to occur. Willingness leads to determination…let our determination be for holiness. All we really want is to reconnect with Holiness…this is our true desire, everything else is just a substitute. The Spirit that is in us, is Us. Our willingness will determine whether we connect to our true identity or to some powerless facsimile. Today, let us focus on bringing our willingness together with the greater power that lies within us. We cannot make ourselves holy, that task was already completed at our creation. We can however renew our awareness of the holy state. A little willingness, linked with the strength of Spirit will bring us into the moment so that we can soon experience reality.

DECEMBER 3 – HAPPY – I am happy. Happiness is our function. Our purpose is to be happy, and to extend happiness to all whom we meet. Spirit will help us convert our suffering into happiness if we ask. The Holy Instant is available to us right now...we can go there whenever we find ourselves caught up in fear or hatred. Do not repress these feelings, rather acknowledge them and then focus on the present moment and allow eternity to cleanse us of these pains. Whenever guilt presents itself, we do not try to alleviate it, but rather give the guilt to Spirit who will purify all of our thinking in this regard. Happiness is our function, it is our gift to give and our gift to receive. Spirit stands ever ready to reveal it to us.

DECEMBER 4 – MIND – I am mind. There is nothing outside ourselves. This radical idea is the key to restoration of sanity. As we observe the seeming wide and diverse world, we see an illusion. The world, the way we see it, is in our thinking. It is a small and pitiful shadow of the real world. The body centered experience that we indulge in is truly a hell of our own making. The kingdom of Heaven is within us…at our core…in the place where we truly live. The world we see is our illusion, Heaven is our reality. There is of course a difference between illusion and reality…by definition, one exists and the other does not. There is nothing outside of us…the world we see does not exist, it is a figment of our imagination. All that exists is Mind, and that is the reality of our own existence and the reality of every living thing. We are Mind.

DECEMBER 5 – GARDEN – I am in the garden. The body cannot know. All of the senses of the body are insufficient to reveal the Truth. Within the small-minded kingdom that you have made there is no room for God. The body has become a fence that restricts and keeps true awareness from entering. A single beam of sunlight has the audacity to call itself the sun…this is suffering indeed. A wave upon the ocean has put itself in a pail at the sea shore and named itself All Water…it grows rank and scum ridden and finally not really fit for life. All of this is unknown to Creation, which continues to see us all well and whole and integrated into the Kingdom. Where we have seen desert lives a garden. Where we notice lack there is naught but plenty. Where we have cried in pain there is only bliss. We are in the garden, dreaming of drought. We are in paradise and yet see destruction. Now is the time to come home, come in from the wars, to stop the conflict and live in Peace. We are in the Garden; we need to put our attention on that.

DECEMBER 6 – LOVE – I am in love. We are in love, of love and all love. Love cannot be learned, it is part of our make-up. Love cannot be acquired through some action, it is freely given and then abundantly received. Our relationship with our fellows is rooted in this love…it is our ultimate connection to all that lives. However, we have been experiencing something quite different. When our lives seem to be in conflict…when we feel at odds with our brothers or just the world in general we have strayed from love. We are directly responsible for our own experience of life. Let us decide today to be in love…this is our heritage and our function. Our function is love…this shows itself in our experience. In the world we give love as forgiveness. In heaven (oneness) we give love as extension (creation). This is our function, to be in love. Relish it.

DECEMBER 7 – HEAL – I am healed. Today, we find healing in all situations by having faith in our brother. Every event seen rightly is a divine opportunity. The body needs no healing; it is only the vagaries of small mind that cause us to think we are sick. In truth, health and wholeness of body relies on seeing it's true purpose and allowing divine mind to use it for that purpose. Our purpose is to find the Good in life and in our fellows. We are healed and we are healers in direct proportion to our faith. Not faith in a superstitious way but rather in the sense of perceiving the truth of God in all living things…to see the Christ in our neighbor…to notice good all around. Acceptance of oneness is the healing of all ills. Unity is our balm and our medicine, harmony is the cure and indeed the healing itself.

DECEMBER 8 – PEACE – I am at peace. Let us examine the barriers to peace so that we can erase them from our thinking. Some of these will come quite clearly from our own twisted desire for chaos; some will seem to be someone else's fault. Our brothers will appear to be uncooperative and the events of the day will conspire to steal our joy. Peace can and will overcome all of these projections. Peace will not beat them into submission, but rather it will embrace every conflict with love and render it like unto itself. From peace we carry a message of love, we are yoked in light with our brothers, ever extending our Fathers kingdom. Happiness and total calm is available to us right now…it already lives deep within us, waiting for our willingness that it might come forth.

DECEMBER 9 – ORDER – I am in divine order. When we recognize that everything is in divine order the peace of God is ours. The problem is that much of the time we desire chaos and conflict. We live in the middle of bliss and yet we put our attention on substitutes that cannot possibly replace it. We are the architects of our own adversity…thinking it be excitement we seek danger and madness. Happily, Spirit lives deep within us and it is always ready to clear away the conflict and show us the truth of our being. All things work together for good, for those who love. Peace flows across whatever obstacle the ego may put in the way, no matter how unfortunate the events of the day seem to be, peace flows across to establish itself as the answer. Today, let us call it forth, releasing our attraction for drama in favor of everlasting love.

DECEMBER 10 – PAINLESS – I am painless. Life is painless when we embrace the love of our Father who is in Heaven. This seems so contrary to the common wisdom… this is so hard to accept. "Life is hard and then you die." This seems to be such an accurate expression of much of our life experience. It need not be this way. All of our pain comes from seeking that which can never satisfy. Body gratification, self- gratification all are attempts to forget our sense of separation. The body has one proper function. This function is communication. We have gotten it mixed up. We have come to believe that we can take our pleasure, reveling in the senses, and not be lonely. We are focused on the thing which divides us and expecting it to heal the separation which it is a creation of…this cannot be. Today, we release guilt and projection and allow peace to flow from within…it fills us, it gifts our brothers, and it heals all pain.

DECEMBER 11 – IMMORTAL – I am immortal. We are filled with life and that life is eternal. We have been tempted to accept the martyrdom of death...thinking it somehow attractive. Singularly unattractive, this insane idea springs from the ego, which has made sin and guilt and death seem inevitable. This is in direct contravention of the laws of God...therefore it cannot be true. God's will is for life and for the continual expansion of life. We are part of the incorruptible body of Christ. This body is not something that we take into our physical body as a way to connect us with God, it is rather our true, immortal self. We do not need symbols to make this real...we are continually in communion with God...this is the eternal truth of our existence. We are immortal.

DECEMBER 12 – FEARLESS – I am fearless. Long, now we have been afraid of God. Leaving God seems to be our greatest sin…surely this is unforgivable. Let us be clear today, we cannot leave God, we cannot turn our back on God, we cannot go anywhere where God is not, we cannot be and never have been apart from God. There is no death, so nothing to fear, there is no judgment, so nothing to regret, there is no payment to be extracted so there is no retribution to fear. The ego fears…it fears for its existence, but we are not our egos. We are of God, in God and integral to God. Our father has nothing but Good for us…He and all the wonders of creation await us just beyond the veil of shadows that we have erroneously woven out of our fear. Today, we make an attempt to take down the shades and let the light shine in.

DECEMBER 13 – SINLESS – I am innocent. Innocence means unaware of sinful things. My brother is innocent; we are all innocent. All throughout this day let us stop comparing our sins, let us release any sense of judgment. "Judge not, that ye be not judged." It means exactly what it says... all judgment comes from us. We can only place a negative judgment on our brother by placing one on ourselves. We have crucified ourselves upon the frame of our perceived sins and we continually call our brother to climb up there with us. Misery's company is a poor substitute for the oneness that is available through forgiveness. Today, let us affirm that we are all sinless. Redeem yourself through the redemption of all those who you have called to judgment. Release the hostages, let them go and be free. Have faith in yourself, have faith in your brother, have faith in God. Embrace our shared perfection and be innocent.

DECEMBER 14 – REMEMBER – I am remembering the light. Creation sings a song of light. Sound and sight combine in this infinite dance of love. All safety lies in our choice to dance the dance of life. We cannot be harmed in any undertaking which moves us into the extension of that which we truly are. Pain is a useless lesson. Our present world is designed to teach through pain. Even when we believe we are victorious we are actually defeated. It is only through the release of all individual goals that we can find the real world and the peace that entails. This does not mean that we resign ourselves to a meager existence, rather it is our greatest calling…to remember that alone we can do nothing and so to attempt nothing alone. All goals should be of spirit and in cooperation with life. Remembering the light means to "Seek first the kingdom…", doing so abundance will be the result.

DECEMBER 15 – RESPONSIBLE – I am responsible for what I see. We are coming to an understanding of how this world works. We are totally responsible for what we see. This may seem to be a difficult acceptance...it does not matter...it is the truth. We choose the feelings that we feel... we decide upon the goal we put our attention on...all the things that seem to happen are only those things which we have asked for. This then is the day when we decide to ask for what we really want. To release suffering and sin is to enter into instant happiness and the accomplishment of the one true goal. Today, let us make our happiness a gift to spirit. When we do this our happiness grows and it becomes our own gift to ourselves and to all of our brothers. Our seeing changes from conflict to harmony...from hell to heaven... and we are then responsible for paradise.

DECEMBER 16 – BELIEF – I am faithful. Faith is the perception we invest in our life events…belief is the story we tell ourselves which confirms our faith…vision is the world we see as a result. We already have all the faith, belief and vision that are needed to enter into the Kingdom of heaven. We only need change how we apply these gifts. Spirit will guide us if we but ask. The way will be made clear for us. Perception will change as we work with the Voice for God as our belief system is unwound. Vision will be restored as the shadows of fear are wiped from our eyes. Endeavor throughout the day to have faith in yourself, in your brother and in God. Remember that these three are really all one and the same. Faith is the medium in which belief leads to vision…remember that.

DECEMBER 17 – OBSERVE – I am observant. Today, let us release all fear to look within. Sometimes we may think that if we look too closely within ourselves that we will find some horror that we cannot bear. It seems easier to look without. We look without and see all of our projected fears reflected back at us in the form of judgment…we judge our brothers as being outside of grace and generally lacking in that which today we believe they should have. We may judge harshly, seeing behavior which is anathema to us. We may judge more positively having a sort of compassion as we observe the suffering of others. All of this is just a distraction from the truth. The truth can only be found within. We must dive down below the surface appearances of life, past the veneer of civilization, past the animal responses of ego, through all of the fears and enter directly into the light that is our spirit. This is the core of Goodness that we find in ourselves and then are able to see in our brother. This vision releases all of us from the chains of sin and sickness. Observe the truth today, see inside.

DECEMBER 18 – SANE -- I am sane. Today, let us choose reason rather than madness. Reason is dedicated to the restoration to sanity. Reason reconnects our will to Goodwill. True reason will not allow any thought of separation because it knows only connectedness. Reason has no weakness for division…it is complete in its ability to see only One. Reason knows only God and sees only God in all things. This is our hope and our cause…to come into this state of mind. Reason allows us to remember that the world we see is a mirror which reflects our choices back to us. Sometimes it seems that our mirror has broken into a million fragments and that then, insanely these fragments have grown arms and legs to fight with one another. Reason is firm and unmoving…discarding this mad vision for the sanity of Heaven. Today, it is reason that we choose.

DECEMBER 19 – ANSWER – I am answered. We call out for the answer to our troubles. Daily we find challenges and sufferings...we ask why. We can use this time today, to find the answer. Our only problem is our sense of separation from Creation...this is the sole cause of all of our maladies, all of our pain and suffering come from this one issue. This sense of aloneness is a lie that we told ourselves. Do you desire to rule your world or be ruled by it? You are son of God; you are indeed ruler of the world you have made. It cannot possibly rule you. You are connected to all Power... so all Power is yours. You have no enemies because all are like you...whole and perfect...without conflict. You cannot sin because you were made innocent. All of these are the answer to the question...but in order to truly accept these words and the true power which lies beyond them we must see that which we have denied. Today, let us work to accept the truth...God is one and we are one with God. This is our answer to all the seeming problems of the world.

DECEMBER 20 – INNER – I am in God. God is in me… God is in us. In God is only joy, only peace, only love, one life…these are not different, indeed they are one. Our words cannot convey the power of this idea. It is only dimly that we can see the full ramifications of these ideas. An inner shift is needed to move us closer the bridge of spirit which stands ready to erase the imaginary distance between us and our father. Reason and order is always in place…no matter how far we seem to have moved from them…they are there to comfort us when we choose again. Happiness is always available, peace is constantly present, love is forever extending…this is the inner reality, this is the truth of our being, which is to say our very existence. Today, shift your attention from the outer madness to our inner reason… embrace the light that always shines within you.

DECEMBER 21 – GLORY – I am in glory. We are in glory. The old idea of being "bound for glory" is not an accurate representation of our path. In truth we are already in Glory. It is only our perception and body identification that keeps us thinking that this is some future destination. This day, we walk in glory, head held high, fearless and sinless. Glory is the ultimate safety. We are unstained by sin and as perfect as ever we were made by God. Where we may have thought we had conflict, let us now recognize that we have been involved in an imaginary war with ourselves. We can call off the campaign and allow ourselves to be unified. Letting go of worry and concern lets us see our fears as baseless and actually returns our attention to love. Today, at every turn let us look for glory…be sure it will be found, for it already is.

DECEMBER 22 – REMEMBER – I am remembering. Today, we attempt a moment of quiet. The deeper we enter into the silence the clearer our memory of God becomes. Our memory of the Holy Parent is totally reliant on our ability to forget what is not of Him. Hence…silence. We release conflict and allow our mind to mend itself. Quickly and quietly we replace viciousness with gentleness. All sense of enmity fades into the light. We need not seek ascendancy because we are already ascendant. The war that never really started is coming to an end. We give ourselves over to God's will, which, of course is our own hidden true will for ourselves. If at any time during the day you feel burdened, remember the presence of God and notice how this burden is instantly and infinitely lighter.

DECEMBER 23 – BROTHER – I am my brother. I am not my brother's keeper, rather, I am my brother. We remember the scripture "If you go to the altar, there to leave your gift, but are angry with your brother go first and be reconciled with your brother and then come back and leave your gift." So many implications…and all of them point to the truth of who our brother really is. He is us and we are him…he is the Christ and therefore our spiritual identity…part of God and in part God. When we go into the quiet and try to commune with spirit, but find that we are distracted by our resentments and regrets we are instructed to go to him or her who seems to be at the center of these feelings. Another aspect is that I cannot quiet the mind if it is filled with grievance. We can however allow the power of Mind heal us from our perceived remorse or regret. We can visualize going to our brother in a peaceful, healing way to resolve the conflict between us. We can feel what it would be like to be in harmony. When we have established this state of mind our peace becomes the gift we offer on the altar.

DECEMBER 24 – TRUTH – I am...in truth. Truth is truth, this is not a matter of perception. We may have believed that we had "our" truth and that others had theirs but this is erroneous on its face. There are no others. All true principle is but an aspect of the One principle...God is one and we are one with God. All aspects of this idea are of equal value just as all parts of God are of equal value. Anytime we believe that some condition is not true for us but that it is true for others, we have strayed. All are equal parts of the integrated kingdom of Heaven. Hear the truth and know that it is...We live and move and have our being in God...as do all living things. That is the Truth and all other true ideas come directly from this, there are no contrary truths.

DECEMBER 25 – SINLESS – I am sinless. Today is a symbolic day of rebirth. We are reborn in Christ consciousness. We are reborn sinless. The idea that everyone sins is not helpful to our unfoldment. "Sinners all" is a hopeless concept that fails to recognize our innate ability to rise above all mistakes and take whatever corrective action is necessary. If we think that missing the mark deserves a death sentence, then we must change our minds accordingly. The escape from the continual cycle of life and death is accomplished by entering into the eternal now. It is in the holy instant that we find revelation which washes away all seeming sin. Let the guilty ones go, release your own shame, be free. As we come into the consciousness of purity and love we come close to our brother and we come closer to God.

DECEMBER 26 – PERFECT – I am perfect? If God be perfect then so must all parts of God be perfect. If we are created by God, then we must be perfect. But if we are prone to mistakes which cause us and others pain, how can we be part of God…or if that is possible then how can we atone for our apparent errors? In Spirit, which is to say in reality, we are all one and we do not make any mistakes. It is only in our body identification that errors are made. To atone for these ego errors, we need only see that they do not exist in reality but only in our perception and that can be changed. We heal the mistakes of the past by seeing that they are like wisps of fog on the morning breeze they dissipate and become invisible before the light of the sun.

DECEMBER 27 – ABUNDANT – I am abundant. We are connected to all the good of universe. There is no lack in creation. We already have all good things because we are a part of all good things. Our desperate fear that those things we have may be taken from us actually keep us from living a prosperous life no matter how much prosperity is evidenced in our experience. Establish abundance in mind by giving freely from yourself. Whatever it is that you have, be willing to give it. Stop grasping and holding on…creation is trying to give you the desires of your heart. Today use your heart, give from the heart and see how immediately your heart is filled…or should we say refilled? We are rich indeed, heir to the kingdom of God. That which God has given can never be taken back, so relax…give and keep giving. All good things are yours to share.

DECEMBER 28 – FEARLESS – I am fearless. In order to be at peace we must let go of all fear. Total peace is that which we seek. It is the gift of Spirit and it is freely given. Today, let us hold nothing more important than the attainment of this gift. Let go of all other goals…there really is nothing to fear…for if we enter into this holy place we can be assured that all good things are already ours. 'Seek first the kingdom and all these will be added to you'. Release any thought of specialness. In the world all try to be special at the expense of others. Even the specialness we assign to others in a left-handed compliment. This is the essence of isolation. Our "specialness" has been our burden all these useless centuries. It has caused all of our fears which have resulted in all of our so-called sins. Our sense of difference is the very state of hell which we seek to escape. Our differences drive us to madness and war, know today that they are figments of our imagination. Here is the truth, in the kingdom there is no reason for specialness because all are wonderful and all are equal and all are therefore at peace.

DECEMBER 29 – FREE – I am free. We are free. Freedom has always been ours, but we have opted to chain ourselves to judgement. Today we continue to practice. Our practice is simple; we see Good in our brother. We will put our attention on the Goodness that stands before us. If at any time you find yourself feeling threatened say to yourself: "My brother and I are one...and we are all one with God." This will set him free and in the process so also will you be free. You have heard it said: "Everyone we meet today has a gift for us and we have one for them. The freedom of spirit to give is the same freedom that in turn creates the universe. Our gifts go forth from us to expand and then return to us somehow multiplied. We will be free to the extent that we are able to grant freedom to those around us. Say it all through the day "I am free...we are free."

DECEMBER 30 - DEFENSELESS – I am defenseless. We need no defense. Today we will change our mind concerning our state of affairs. In our chosen loneliness we seemingly have much to fear and much to lose. We have painted a world of threat onto the canvas of our thoughts. It is enough, let us turn from thoughts of difference and division. We can put our perception to work for the good of our very being. Seeing situations as dangerous, or seeing our brothers threatening causes one conflict after another. They become a chain of effects issuing from a nonexistent cause. Sometimes it seems like we should take up the cause against some force or some person…this cause is doomed. There is only one Cause and that is our Holy Parent. Any other cause which we think exists or which we think to take up is just a distraction from the truth. If there is no threat, then we do not have to defend. We can be "for" the Good and release all sense of evil. This is what Jesus meant when he said "Resist not evil". Stand for Something, be against nothing and the offense of defense will not occur.

DECEMBER 31 – CHRIST – I am anointed. We are the Christ. All of us anointed in the Spirit. We are of the Universe, children of Creation, Son of God; this is our true existence. Our dream of uniqueness has stolen our inheritance from us. Alone we do nothing, together we not only accomplish all things, but we are all things. The Christ in us forgives instantly, it recognizes that the only thing of value is Love and it extends that love through us. There is no danger here… we walk together in the light of God. Get quiet for a time, this holy presence is the very essence of stillness. Reach for it right now, take on the shining mantle that is your birthright. Cover yourself in this cloak of light and love. Allow it to enfold you…after a few moments you will come to see that you also enfold it. As within so without…you are anointed and you anoint. "Let the mind that was in Christ Jesus be in you." This is a call of permission, for God will not force anything upon us. We must allow this mind to be active in us and when we do we realize it was really ours all along.

Printed in the United States
By Bookmasters